Contents

Y053771

BEST BISCUITS

Editor **Liberty Mendez**

BBC Books, an imprint of Ebury Publishing
20 Vauxhall Bridge Road,
London SW1V 2SA

BBC Books is part of the Penguin Random House group of companies whose addresses can be found at global.penguinrandomhouse.com

Photographs © BBC Magazines 2022
Recipes © BBC Worldwide 2022
Book design © Woodlands Books Ltd 2022

All recipes contained in this book first appeared in *BBC Good Food magazine*.

First published by BBC Books in 2022

www.penguin.co.uk

A CIP catalogue record for this book is available from the British Library

ISBN 9781785947865

Printed and bound in Latvia, by Livonia Print

Project editors: Nell Warner and Kay Halsey
Design: Interstate Creative Partners Ltd and Peppis Designworks
Cover Design: Two Associates
Production: Catherine Ngwong
Picture Researcher: Gabby Harrington

Penguin Random House is committed to a sustainable
future for our business, our readers and our planet. This
book is made from Forest Stewardship Council® certified paper.

PICTURE AND RECIPE CREDITS

BBC Books would like to thank the following people for providing photos. While every effort has been made to trace and acknowledge all photographers, we should like to apologise should there be any errors or omissions.

Peter Cassidy p23, p31, p45, p47, p59, p67, p109, p165; Mike English p27, p61, p75, p79, p81, p83, p93, p101, p115, p121, p125, p137, p139, p149, p191, p195, p201, p203, p209; Will Heap p37, p39, p95, p177, p205; Lara Holmes p131; Adrian Lawrence p183; David Munns p55, p57, p63, p65, p85, p97, p135, p143, p147, p155, p163, p169; Myles New p77, p133, p141, p179; Stuart Ovenden p33, p35, p113, p129, p145, p153, p157; Lis Parsons p69; Tom Regester p25, p41, p49, p103, p105, p111, p181; Toby Scott p127; Roger Stowell p161, p175; Sam Stowell p51, p53, p87, p89, p91, p159, p173, p185, p189, p199, p207; Rob Streeter p13, p29, p43, p73, p99, p117, p123, p151; Philip Webb p71, p171, p193; Clare Winfield p11, p15, p17, p19, p21, p187

All the recipes in this book were created by the editorial team at *Good Food* and by regular contributors to BBC Magazines.

Introduction

What makes up your ultimate biscuit? Buttery and loaded with chocolate chips, or perhaps you prefer a softer savoury biscuit with crumbly cheese and toasty nuts. No matter what your favourite biscuit may be, you will find something in this little, yet mighty, book to satisfy your biscuit needs.

It's full of the fail-proof biscuit recipes that you always wished you had up your sleeve, suitable for any occasion. All the recipes have been tested in the *Good Food* test kitchen, so you can guarantee success with every biscuit you bake.

Whether you're new to baking or want a challenge, you'll find something to satisfy your culinary needs here. From classic caramelised Florentines to the more experimental Saffron, pistachio &

white chocolate cookies, there's a biscuit for everyone. If you are looking for something to dip into your cup of tea, I urge you to try our classic biscuit tin recipes. You'll find everything from a rich bourbon biscuit to a melt-in-your-mouth shortbread. Not only are you getting bakes that you can use for occasions like Christmas and Valentine's Day, but there is also a host of our favourite timeless recipes, vegan and gluten-free biscuits and even a whole chapter on cookies.

Enjoy baking!

Liberty Mendez, Editor

Notes & conversion tables

NOTES ON THE RECIPES
- Eggs are large in the UK and Australia and extra large in America unless stated.
- Wash fresh produce before preparation.
- Recipes contain nutritional analyses for 'sugars', which means the total sugar content, including all natural sugars in the ingredients, unless otherwise stated.

APPROXIMATE WEIGHT CONVERSIONS
Cup measurements, which are used in Australia and America, have not been listed here as they vary from ingredient to ingredient. Kitchen scales should be used to measure dry/solid ingredients.

Good Food cares about sustainable sourcing and animal welfare. Where possible, free-range eggs have been used when recipes were originally tested.

OVEN TEMPERATURES

GAS	°C	°C FAN	°F	OVEN TEMP.
¼	110	90	225	Very cool
½	120	100	250	Very cool
1	140	120	275	Cool or slow
2	150	130	300	Cool or slow
3	160	140	325	Warm
4	180	160	350	Moderate
5	190	170	375	Moderately hot
6	200	180	400	Fairly hot
7	220	200	425	Hot
8	230	210	450	Very hot
9	240	220	475	Very hot

SPOON MEASURES

Spoon measurements are level unless otherwise specified.

- 1 teaspoon (tsp) = 5ml
- 1 tablespoon (tbsp) = 15ml
- 1 Australian tablespoon = 20ml (cooks in Australia should measure 3 teaspoons where 1 tablespoon is specified in a recipe)

APPROXIMATE LIQUID CONVERSIONS

METRIC	IMPERIAL	AUS	US
50ml	2fl oz	¼ cup	¼ cup
125ml	4fl oz	½ cup	½ cup
175ml	6fl oz	¾ cup	¾ cup
225ml	8fl oz	1 cup	1 cup
300ml	10fl oz/½ pint	½ pint	1¼ cups
450ml	16fl oz	2 cups	2 cups/1 pint
600ml	20fl oz/1 pint	1 pint	2½ cups
1 litre	35fl oz/1¾ pints	1¾ pints	1 quart

Chapter 1

CLASSIC BISCUIT TIN BISCUITS

Sometimes there's nothing better than a classic – a traditional biscuit that you go back for time and time again. The kind of biscuit that the family fight over and that is the first to go from the biscuit tin. Whatever your favourite may be, I hope you enjoy our selection of biscuit tin classics.

Basic biscuit dough

This biscuit dough can be used to make all kinds of shaped and iced biscuits. Use it as a vanilla base or flavour – we've given you some suggestions under the recipe.

 PREP 10 mins MAKES 25–30

- 300g plain flour, plus extra for dusting
- 150g white or golden caster sugar
- 150g slightly salted butter, chopped
- 1 large egg
- 2 tsp vanilla extract or vanilla bean paste
- 1–2 tbsp milk

1 Weigh the flour and sugar and put them in a large bowl. Add the butter and rub it into the flour mixture with your fingertips until the mixture resembles wet sand; there should be no buttery lumps.

2 Beat the egg with the vanilla, then add the mixture to the bowl with the milk. Mix everything briefly with a cutlery knife to combine the egg with the dry ingredients, then use your hands to knead the dough together – try not to overwork the dough or the biscuits will be tough. Shape the dough into a disc, then wrap and chill for at least 30 mins before cutting out the biscuits.

FLAVOURINGS

Citrus: Add the zest of an orange, lime or lemon instead of the vanilla. Stir the zest into the egg. For a stronger flavour, use 2 limes.

Cinnamon: Add a large pinch of cinnamon to the flour when you weigh it out, adding the vanilla as well.

Chocolate: Swap 40g flour for 40g cocoa powder. Add a splash of milk if the mixture is too dry to bring together at the end.

Nutrition per serving
energy 98 kcals, fat 5g, saturates 3g, carbs 13g, sugars 5g, fibre 0.4g, protein 1g, salt 0.1g

Shortbread biscuits

Make these moreish shortbread biscuits using just three ingredients. They're wonderfully crumbly and go perfectly with a cup of tea for a mid-morning delight.

 PREP 20 mins COOK 20 mins MAKES 20

- 150g plain flour, plus extra for dusting
- 100g butter, chilled and cubed
- 50g caster sugar, plus 1 tbsp for sprinkling

1 Heat the oven 170C/150C fan/gas 3. Put the flour, butter and sugar into a mixing bowl. Use your hands to combine the ingredients until the mixture looks like breadcrumbs, then squeeze until it comes together as a dough.

2 On a lightly floured surface, use a rolling pin to roll out the dough to ½ cm thick. Cut the dough into fingers and place on a lined baking tray. Use a fork to create imprints, then sprinkle with the remaining caster sugar.

3 Chill the dough in the fridge for 20 mins, then bake for 15–20 mins until golden brown. Remove the shortbread fingers from the oven and leave to cool on the tray for 10 mins.

Nutrition per serving
energy 79 kcals, fat 4g, saturates 3g, carbs 9g, sugars 4g, fibre 0.3g, protein 1g, salt 0.1g

Ginger biscuits

Use fresh and ground ginger to make these spiced biscuits. They're a biscuit tin classic and taste even better being homemade.

 PREP 20 mins COOK 10 mins   MAKES 20

- 100g salted butter, cubed
- 75g light brown soft sugar
- 1 tbsp grated fresh ginger
- 100g golden syrup
- 250g self-raising flour
- 1½ tbsp ground ginger
- 1 tsp bicarbonate of soda
- 1 small egg yolk, beaten

1 Heat the oven to 190C/170C fan/gas 5. Line two large baking trays with parchment. In a saucepan over a low heat, melt the butter, sugar, fresh ginger and golden syrup and leave to cool.

2 Mix the flour, ground ginger and bicarbonate of soda together in a bowl with a wooden spoon. Gradually stir in the cooled sugar mixture and the egg yolk and knead briefly to make a dough.

3 Roll the dough into 20g balls and put on the prepared baking trays with about 3cm between each to allow for spreading. Bake for 8–10 mins until golden brown. Leave to cool on the trays for a min, then transfer to a rack to cool completely.

Nutrition per serving
energy 117 kcals, fat 5g, saturates 3g, carbs 17g, sugars 8g, fibre 1g, protein 1g, salt 0.3g

Bourbon biscuits

Add some colour to classic bourbon biscuits using pink food colouring. Kids will love piping the filling – and eating them afterwards of course!

 PREP 40 mins + freezing COOK 10 mins   MAKES 25

- 125g soft unsalted butter
- 125g golden caster sugar, plus extra for sprinkling
- 2 tbsp golden syrup
- 1 large egg, lightly beaten
- 250g plain flour, plus extra for dusting
- 50g cocoa powder
- 1 tsp baking powder

FOR THE FILLING
- 150g unsalted butter, softened
- 360g icing sugar, sifted
- 4 tbsp cocoa powder
- pink food colouring

1 Beat the butter and sugar until creamy, then mix in the rest of the ingredients to form a dough, adding a splash of milk if dry.

2 Line three baking sheets, dust with flour, then roll and pat one-third of the dough out to the thickness of a £1 coin on each. Cover and freeze for 15 mins.

3 Heat the oven to 180C/160C fan/gas 4. Slide off the trays and cover with parchment. Trim edges to straighten, then cut in 6cm x 3cm rectangles. Lift onto the trays, leaving space between. Use a cocktail stick to make the pricked pattern (not too many or they'll break). Put back in the freezer if it gets soft.

4 Bake for 8–10 mins, then cool on the sheet. Sprinkle over some sugar.

5 Beat the butter and icing sugar together, then divide into three. Add cocoa to one, a dot of pink to another and leave the last plain (add more sugar if needed). Spoon into piping or sandwich bags with the corner snipped off.

6 Pipe the icings onto half, sandwich with the other halves and leave to set.

Nutrition per serving
energy 221 kcals, fat 10g, saturates 6g, carbs 29g, sugars 21g, fibre 1g, protein 2g, salt 0.08g

Oat biscuits

Nothing beats homemade cookies – make these easy oat biscuits for a sweet treat during the day when you need a break.

 PREP 15 mins COOK 15 mins   MAKES 10 large biscuits or 15 medium ones

- 75g wholemeal flour
- 1 tsp baking powder
- 75g porridge oats
- 50g caster sugar
- 75g butter
- 1 tbsp golden syrup
- 2 tbsp milk

1 Heat the oven to 180C/160C fan/gas 4. Line a baking tray with parchment. Sift the flour into a bowl. Mix in the baking powder, porridge oats and sugar.

2 Melt the butter, syrup and milk in a small saucepan or in the microwave and stir. Add to the dry ingredients. Mix until the liquid covers all the oat mixture and until well combined.

3 Spoon onto a baking tray and shape into rounds, leaving space between each biscuit as they will spread whilst cooking. Bake for 10–15 mins, or until golden brown. Leave to cool for 5 mins before removing from tray.

Nutrition per serving
energy 140 kcals, fat 7g, saturates 4g, carbs 17g, sugars 7g, fibre 1g, protein 2g, salt 0.3g

Vanilla biscuits

The simplest biscuits you will ever bake. We've stamped different toys into these to decorate them – try your own favourite patterns.

🕐 PREP 10 mins COOK 10 mins 🥧 MAKES 24

- 200g unsalted butter, softened
- 200g golden caster sugar
- 1 large egg
- ½ tsp vanilla extract
- 400g plain flour, plus extra for dusting

YOU WILL NEED
- 9cm cookie cutters

1 Heat the oven to 200C/180C fan/gas 6 and line a baking sheet with parchment. Put the butter in a bowl and beat with electric beaters until soft and creamy. Beat in the sugar, then the egg and vanilla, and finally the flour to make a dough. If the dough feels sticky, add a little flour and knead it in.

2 Pull pieces off the dough and roll them out to about the thickness of two £1 coins on a floured surface. The easiest way to do this is to roll the mixture out on a baking mat. Cut out shapes using cookie cutters or a use the rim of a small glass and peel away the leftover dough around the edges. Press some clean toys gently into the biscuits, making sure you make enough of a mark without going all the way through. Re-roll off-cuts and repeat.

3 Transfer the whole mat or the individual biscuits to the sheet and bake for 8–10 mins or until the edges are just brown. Cool for 5 mins, then serve. Will keep for 3 days in a tin.

Nutrition per serving
energy 161 kcals, fat 7g, saturates 4g, carbs 21g, sugars 8g, fibre 1g, protein 2g, salt 0g

Simple jammy biscuits

Fill these biscuits with your favourite jam. We used strawberry, but raspberry or even blackcurrant work well!

 PREP 10 mins COOK 15 mins   SERVES 12

- 200g self-raising flour
- 100g caster sugar
- 100g butter
- 1 egg, lightly beaten
- 4 tbsp strawberry jam

1 Heat the oven to 190C/170C fan/gas 5. Rub the flour, sugar and butter together until the mixture resembles breadcrumbs. Alternatively, you can do this in the food processor. Add enough egg to bring the mixture together to form a stiff dough.

2 Flour your hands and shape the dough into a tube, about 5cm in diameter. Cut into 2cm-thick slices and place on a large baking sheet. Space them out as the mixture will spread when baking.

3 Make a small indentation in the middle of each slice with the end of a wooden spoon and drop a tsp of jam in the centre. Bake for 10–15 mins until slightly risen and just golden. Cool on a rack.

Nutrition per serving
energy 170 kcals, fat 8g, saturates 5g, carbs 25g, sugars 13g, fibre 0.5g, protein 2g, salt

Anzac biscuits

These iconic biscuits were originally made to send to the ANZACs (Australian and New Zealand Army Corps) serving in Gallipoli.

 PREP 10 mins COOK 15 mins   MAKES 20

- 85g porridge oats
- 85g desiccated coconut
- 100g plain flour
- 100g caster sugar
- 100g butter, plus extra butter for greasing
- 1 tbsp golden syrup
- 1 tsp bicarbonate of soda

1 Heat the oven to 180C/160C fan/gas 4. Put the oats, coconut, flour and sugar in a bowl. Melt the butter in a small pan and stir in the golden syrup. Add the bicarbonate of soda to 2 tbsp boiling water, then stir into the golden syrup and butter mixture.

2 Make a well in the middle of the dry ingredients and pour in the butter and golden syrup mixture. Stir gently to incorporate the dry ingredients.

3 Put dessert spoonfuls of the mixture on to buttered baking sheets, about 2.5cm apart to allow room for spreading. Bake in batches for 8–10 mins until golden. Transfer to a rack to cool.

Nutrition per serving
energy 118 kcals, fat 7g, saturates 5g, carbs 13g, sugars 6g, fibre 1g, protein 1g, salt 0.28g

Chapter 2

COOKIES

. . . .

A golden chocolate chip cookie, dotted with molten chocolate chips, which is crisp on the outside and soft in the middle, is a dream. Biting into a nutty cookie bursting with toasty flavours is a delight. Here's a selection of our favourite cookie recipes. There's everything from traditional flavour combinations like mint choc chip to butterscotch ones, from cookies for the more adventurous palate to classic flavour combinations. There's something for everyone!

Saffron, pistachio & white choc cookies

Add saffron to your cookie dough and you'll be bang on trend. Pistachio and white chocolate are great additions too. One biscuit just won't be enough.

 PREP 15 mins + chilling COOK 20 mins   MAKES 12–15

- 30ml milk
- big pinch saffron
- 220g butter, melted
- 1 large egg
- 100g golden caster sugar
- 100g light brown soft sugar
- 300g plain flour
- ½ tsp baking powder
- 200g white chocolate
- 100g pistachios, roughly chopped

1 Warm the milk in a pan with the saffron. Once steaming, take off the heat and whisk in the butter, then chill in the fridge. Whisk the egg with the caster sugar until light and fluffy – this will take around 3–5 mins, then add the cooled butter and brown sugar and whisk briefly to combine. Tip in the flour, baking powder and a big pinch of salt and use a spatula or paddle attachment of a stand mixer to combine, without overmixing.

2 Fold in the chocolate and pistachios, then tip onto parchment. Roll up into a thick, compact log and twist the ends to make a cracker shape. Wrap in cling film, then chill in the fridge for a couple of hours or overnight.

3 Heat the oven to 190C/170C fan/gas 5 and line a baking sheet with parchment. Unwrap the log and slice into 1cm discs, space out on the sheet (you might need to do this in two batches) and bake for 12–15 mins until set and golden around the edges, but soft. Cool a little, then move to a rack to cool completely. Will keep for 2–3 days in an airtight container.

Nutrition per serving
energy 352 kcals, fat 20g, saturates 11g, carbs 37g, sugars 21g, fibre 1g, protein 5g, salt 0.4g

Chewy chocolate chip cookies

Enjoy these chewy chocolate chip cookies with a cup of tea. If you have time, leave the dough overnight for the best flavour and texture.

 PREP 10 mins + optional overnight chilling COOK 10 mins  MAKES 12

- 150g butter, softened
- 150g soft brown sugar, golden caster sugar or ideally half of each
- 1 egg
- 1 tsp vanilla extract
- 180–200g plain flour
- ½ tsp baking powder
- 200g chocolate chips or chopped chocolate

1 Mix the butter and sugar together using an electric whisk or hand whisk until very light and fluffy, then beat in the egg and vanilla. Quickly fold in the flour, baking powder, chocolate and ¼ tsp salt. Don't overwork the dough as this will toughen the cookies.

2 For the best flavour, leave the mixture overnight: either cover the bowl and chill, or roll the mixture into balls and chill.

3 Heat the oven to 180C/160C fan/gas 4 and line two baking sheets with parchment. Divide the mixture into balls, the craggier the balls, the rougher the cookies will look. If you want to give the dough more texture, tear the balls in half and squidge them lightly back together. Space out evenly on the baking sheets, leaving space between each.

4 Bake the fresh cookies for 8–10 mins and the chilled for 10–12 mins, or until brown and crisp at the edges but still very soft in the middle. Cool on the tray for a few minutes before eating or transfer to a rack to cool completely. Keeps for 3 days in an airtight container.

Nutrition per serving
energy 299 kcals, fat 17g, saturates 10g, carbs 31g, sugars 18g, fibre 2g, protein 3g, salt 0.4g

Peanut butter cookie cups

Pair the winning combination of peanut butter and dark chocolate in these cookie cups. They're perfect for a picnic or pick-me-up treat for the whole family.

 PREP 25 mins + setting   COOK 18 mins   MAKES 12

- 175g butter, softened
- 200g light brown soft sugar
- 100g golden caster sugar
- 1 tbsp vanilla extract
- 1 large egg
- 250g plain flour
- ½ tsp bicarbonate of soda
- 150g dark chocolate (at least 70% cocoa solids)
- 240g peanut or almond butter

1 Heat the oven to 190C/170C fan/gas 5. Tip the butter, sugars and vanilla into a bowl and beat with an electric whisk until pale and fluffy. Beat in the egg. Add the flour, bicarb and a pinch of salt, and mix everything together with a spatula.

2 Break off golf-ball-sized lumps of dough (about 65g each) and press into the holes of a 12-hole muffin tin, ensuring they comes up the sides (if you're using a deep muffin tin, the dough should come halfway up). Bake for 15 mins until golden. The dough will sink as it bakes, so leave until cool enough to handle, then press it up the sides again. Leave to cool.

3 Break the chocolate into a heatproof bowl and melt until smooth in the microwave or set over a pan of barely simmering water, ensuring the bowl doesn't touch the water. Remove the cookie cups from the tin using a cutlery knife to help you. Spoon 1 tsp nut butter into the centres, then cover with the chocolate. Leave to set for 1 hr. Keeps in an airtight container for 5 days.

Nutrition per serving
energy 492 kcals, fat 28g, saturates 13g, carbs 48g, sugars 29g, fibre 3g, protein 9g, salt 0.6g

Next-level chocolate chip cookies

Forget brittle packet versions and make these ultimate choc chip cookies. Expect a crisp exterior, chewy middle and chunks of gooey dark chocolate.

 PREP 20 mins + chilling COOK 20 mins   MAKES 12

- 125g unsalted butter
- 100g plain flour
- 100g rye flour
- 1 tsp sea salt flakes, plus extra for sprinkling
- 1 tsp baking powder
- ¼ tsp bicarbonate of soda
- 200g light brown soft sugar
- 100g golden caster sugar
- 1 large egg, plus 2 large yolks
- 1 tsp vanilla extract
- 200g chocolate, chopped into small chunks (choose dark or milk, or a mixture of the two)

1 Melt the butter in a pan until sizzling. Watch carefully – the butter will foam, and then will turn hazelnut brown. At this point, remove from the heat, tip in a bowl and cool. Mix the flours, salt, baking powder and bicarb in a bowl.

2 Tip the sugars into the butter and beat with a wooden spoon. Add the egg, yolks and vanilla and beat. Scrape the wet mixture into the dry ingredients and stir until it forms a dough. Fold in the chocolate, then chill for at least 3 hrs, or until firm. Will keep chilled for up to 24 hrs.

3 Heat the oven to 180C/160C fan/gas 4. Line two large baking sheets with parchment. Separate the dough into 12 pieces and roll into balls, then put six balls on each sheet, leaving space between them. Bake for 10 mins, then, one sheet at a time, remove from the oven, sprinkle with sea salt and slam the sheet hard against your work surface.

4 Bake for another 3 mins, then repeat the slamming. Bake for 3 mins more or a little longer if you prefer firmer cookies. Cool on the sheets for 10 mins, then transfer to a rack.

Nutrition per serving
energy 346 kcals, fat 16g, saturates 9g, carbs 44g, sugars 31g, fibre 3g, protein 4g, salt 0.7g

Maple, pecan & raisin oaty cookies

Keep these chewy cookies in the freezer ready for when friends or family pop around. The perfect mix of toasty pecans and sweet raisins.

 PREP 20 mins COOK 16 mins   MAKES 18

- 140g rolled oats
- 50g desiccated coconut
- 225g plain flour
- 140g salted pecans, roughly chopped
- 100g raisins
- 140g unsalted butter
- 225g light brown soft sugar
- 3 tbsp maple syrup
- 3 tbsp golden syrup
- 2 tbsp boiling water
- 1 tsp bicarbonate of soda

1 Heat the oven to 160C/140C fan/gas 3. Line three large baking trays with parchment. In a medium bowl, mix the oats, coconut, flour, pecans and raisins. Set aside.

2 In a small saucepan, melt the butter and sugar with the syrups, then remove from the heat. Combine the boiling water and bicarb, then add this to the butter mix. Pour over the oat mixture and stir to combine. Form balls using an ice-cream scoop of mixture and place on the lined trays, with lots of space around them, about six per tray. Flatten each ball slightly.

3 Bake for 14–16 mins, depending on how chewy you like them. Allow to stand for 1 min then transfer to a rack to cool. Keep in an airtight container for up to 1 week, or freeze for up to 3 months.

Nutrition per serving
energy 279 kcals, fat 15g, saturates 6g, carbs 36g, sugars 20g, fibre 2g, protein 3g, salt 0.27g

Lighter double chocolate chip cookies

Enjoy these lighter, yet still chocolatey, cookies with just 97 calories per biscuit.

 PREP 25 mins + cooling + firming COOK 12 mins MAKES 22

- 85g butter
- 1 tbsp cocoa powder
- 1 tsp instant coffee granules
- 85g light muscovado sugar
- 25g golden granulated sugar
- 85g dark chocolate (about 70% cocoa solids)
- 1 medium egg, beaten
- ½ tsp vanilla extract
- 140g plain flour
- ½ tsp bicarbonate of soda

1 Line a couple of baking sheets with parchment. Put the butter, cocoa and coffee in a medium saucepan then heat gently until the butter has melted. Remove from the heat, stir in both the sugars, then leave to cool.

2 Chop the chocolate into small pieces. Beat the egg and vanilla into the cooled butter mix to make a smooth batter. Stir the flour and bicarbonate of soda together. Tip it into the batter mixture with two-thirds of the chocolate, then gently stir together to combine. Don't overmix. Leave for 10–15 mins to firm up slightly, ready for shaping. Heat the oven to 180C/160C fan/gas 4.

3 Using your hands, shape the mixture into 22 small balls. Lay on the lined sheets, well apart so they have room to spread (you may have to bake in batches). Press the rest of the chocolate pieces on top of each cookie. Can be frozen on sheets and then transferred to bags at this stage for up to 1 month. Bake for 12 mins. Leave on the sheets for a couple of mins, then transfer to a rack.

Nutrition per serving
energy 97 kcals, fat 5g, saturates 3g, carbs 12g, sugars 6g, fibre 1g, protein 1g, salt 0.12g

Peanut butter jelly cookies

Enjoy the classic American combo of peanut butter and 'jelly' in a cookie. We used raspberry jam but you can make it your own by using your favourite flavour.

 PREP 20 mins COOK 12 mins   MAKES 10

- 70g butter, softened
- 50g peanut butter
- 75g light brown sugar
- 75g golden caster sugar
- 1 medium egg
- 1 tsp vanilla extract
- 180g plain flour
- 2 tbsp chopped peanuts
- ½ tsp bicarbonate of soda
- 10 heaped tsp raspberry jam

1 Heat the oven to 180C/160C fan/ gas 4 and line two baking sheets with parchment. Cream the butter, peanut butter and sugars together until very light and fluffy, then beat in the egg and vanilla. Once combined, stir in the flour, chopped peanuts, bicarb and ¼ tsp salt.

2 Scoop 10 large tbsp of the mixture onto the trays, leaving enough space between each to allow for spreading. Make a thumbprint in the centre of the cookies and fill each with 1 heaped tsp jam. Bake for 10–12 mins or until firm at the edges but still soft in the middle – they will harden a little as they cool. Leave to cool on the tray for a few mins before eating warm, or transfer to a rack to cool completely. Will keep for 3 days in an airtight container.

Nutrition per serving
energy 250 kcals, fat 11g, saturates 5g, carbs 33g, sugars 19g, fibre 1g, protein 5g, salt 0.49g

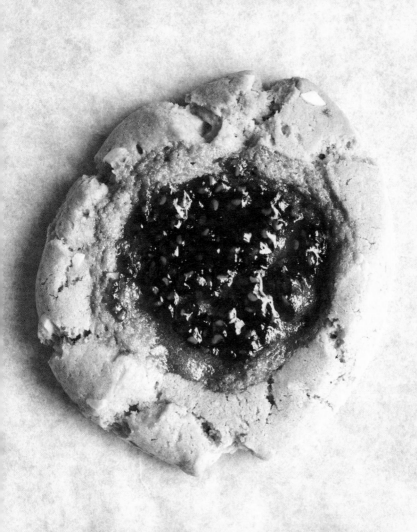

Mint chocolate chip cookies

Mint choc chip isn't just for ice cream! These chocolate chip cookies are made with little pieces of peppermint candy canes for an extra flourish – perfect for the festive season.

 PREP 15 mins + chilling COOK 14 mins   SERVES 16

- 125g salted butter
- 125g light brown soft sugar
- 100g caster sugar
- 1 large egg
- 225g plain flour
- ½ tsp baking powder
- 2 drops peppermint extract
- 100g dark chocolate chips
- 100g dark chocolate, roughly chopped
- 3 peppermint candy canes, finely chopped or crushed

1 Melt the butter in a pan, leave to cool for a few minutes, then pour into a bowl. Whisk in both sugars and the egg until combined.

2 Use a wooden spoon to mix in the flour and baking powder and form a dough. Beat in the peppermint extract, then fold in the chocolate chips. Wrap well and chill for 1 hr.

3 Heat the oven to 180C/160C fan/gas 4. Divide the dough into 16 balls (45g each). Arrange on two baking trays lined with parchment, well-spaced apart, and press down slightly. Bake for 10 mins, then remove from the oven and tap the trays sharply on a work surface to flatten the cookies. Return to the oven and repeat this after 2 mins, then again after another 2 mins (bake for 14 mins in total). Cool completely on the trays.

4 Melt the chocolate in a heatproof bowl over a pan of simmering water or in the microwave. Line a baking tray with parchment. Dip one half of each cookie in the chocolate, place on the tray and sprinkle with candy cane. Transfer to the fridge for 30 mins to set.

Nutrition per serving
energy 252 kcals, fat 12g, saturates 7g, carbs 31g, sugars 19g, fibre 2g, protein 3g, salt 0.2g

Hazelnut & chocolate cookie sandwiches

How do you make chocolate chip cookies even better? Stuff them with chocolate! These hazelnut & chocolate cookie sandwiches are the ultimate indulgence.

 PREP 20 mins + cooling COOK 12 mins   MAKES 12

- 120g unsalted butter, softened
- 100g light brown soft sugar
- 75g golden caster sugar
- ½ tsp fine sea salt
- 1 medium egg, lightly beaten
- 1 tsp vanilla extract
- 200g plain flour
- ¼ tsp bicarbonate of soda
- 100g milk chocolate, roughly chopped
- 70g skinless hazelnuts, roughly chopped and toasted
- 120g chocolate hazelnut spread

1 Heat the oven to 200C/180C fan/gas 6. Line two baking sheets with parchment.
2 Cream the butter with both sugars in a large mixing bowl using an electric whisk, then beat in the salt, egg and vanilla. Stir in the flour, bicarbonate of soda, chocolate and hazelnuts using a wooden spoon until well combined.
3 Scoop the dough onto the baking sheets in 24 heaps, well spaced apart. Bake for 10–12 mins or until lightly golden at the edges. Remove from the oven and allow to cool completely on the baking sheets. Spread 1 tsp of chocolate spread on the bottoms of half the cookies, then sandwich with the other halves. Will keep in a cake tin or airtight container for up to 5 days.

Nutrition per serving
energy 336 kcals, fat 18g, saturates 8g, carbs 37g, sugars 24g, fibre 2g, protein 4g, salt 0.5g

Choc chip cookie ice cream sandwiches

Kids can help cook these chewy American-style biscuits – use two of them to squish vanilla ice cream into a hand-held treat.

 PREP 20 mins + overnight chilling COOK 20 mins   MAKES 12 sandwiches or 24 cookies

- 280g light brown soft sugar
- 225g granulated sugar
- 250g butter
- 2 large eggs
- 1 tbsp vanilla extract
- 450g plain flour
- 2 tsp baking powder
- 300g good-quality milk chocolate, roughly chopped into chunks
- vanilla ice cream, to serve

1 To make the cookies, tip the sugars and butter into a bowl. Use an electric hand mixer to blend until smooth, creamy and paler.

2 Break in the eggs, one at a time, mixing well between each and pausing to scrape down the sides with a spatula. Mix in the vanilla.

3 Sift in the flour and baking powder, then mix well with a wooden spoon. Stir through the chocolate chunks. Use your hands to squeeze the dough together, then split in two. Put each piece on a sheet of cling film.

4 Roll each piece of dough in the cling film so that they form thick sausage shapes, then seal the ends. Chill for at least 3 hrs or overnight – they can be frozen at this point.

5 Heat the oven to 180C/160C fan/gas 4. Take the rolls out of the fridge, unwrap and slice each one into 12 pieces, so you have 24 in total. Place the slices on a baking tray lined with parchment. Bake for 20 mins until golden brown on the edges, but pale in the centre.

6 Cool slightly before lifting onto a rack to cool completely. Sandwich with ice cream.

Nutrition per serving
energy 623 kcals, fat 28g, saturates 17g, carbs 85g, sugars 59g, fibre 2g, protein 7g, salt 0.7g

Pistachio & cranberry cookies

These crunchy fruit & nut biscuits are sure to be a family favourite - make ahead and freeze, or wrap up for the perfect homemade gift.

PREP 15 mins + chilling COOK 15 mins   MAKES 22

- 175g butter, softened
- 85g golden caster sugar
- ½ tsp vanilla extract
- 225g plain flour
- 75g pistachios
- 75g dried cranberries

1 Mix the butter, sugar and vanilla extract with a wooden spoon. Stir in the flour, then tip in the pistachios and cranberries – you might need to get your hands in at this stage to bring the mix together as a dough. Halve the dough and shape each half into a log about 5cm across. Wrap in cling film, then chill for 1 hr or freeze for up to 3 months.

2 Heat the oven to 180C/160C fan/gas 4. Slice the logs into 1cm-thick rounds, place on a baking tray lined with parchment and bake for 12–15 mins. Cool completely on the tray.

Nutrition per serving
energy 140 kcals, fat 9g, saturates 4g, carbs 15g, sugars 7g, fibre 0g, protein 2g, salt 0.1g

Butterscotch cookies

Hidden rice puffs give these butterscotch chocolate chip biscuits a good crunch and take them to the next level.

 PREP 10 mins COOK 20 mins   MAKES 10

- 100g light brown soft sugar
- 2 tbsp golden syrup
- 175g self-raising flour
- 25g puffed rice cereal
- dark chocolate chips,
  for decoration

1 Heat the oven to 160C/140C fan/gas 3. In a large bowl, beat together the butter, sugar and golden syrup until smooth.

2 Sift in the flour and mix, then fold through the puffed rice cereal. Roll into walnut-sized balls and place, well-spaced, on a baking sheet lined with parchment. Decorate each ball with a few chocolate chips.

3 Bake for 15–20 mins until golden. Leave on the baking sheet for 1 min before removing to a rack to cool.

Nutrition per serving
energy 188 kcals, fat 8g, saturates 5g, carbs 27g, sugars 13g, fibre 1g, protein 2g, salt 0.2g

Raspberry & almond breakfast cookies

Grab a few of these energy-boosting cookies for a quick breakfast or offer as snacks to bridge the hunger gap before dinner. Enjoy with yogurt and fruit.

PREP 10 mins   COOK 15 mins   MAKES 12

- 2 ripe bananas, mashed
- 150g porridge oats
- 2 tbsp ground almonds
- ½ tsp cinnamon
- 100g raspberries (fresh or frozen)

1 Heat the oven to 200C/180C fan/gas 6 and line two baking trays with parchment. Mix the banana, oats, almonds, cinnamon and a pinch of salt in a bowl to make a sticky dough. Gently stir through the raspberries, trying not to break them up. Scoop up tablespoons of the mixture and roll into balls, then place on a baking tray and flatten with your hand.

2 Bake for 15 mins until the cookies feel firm around the edges and are golden brown. Leave to cool. Will keep in an airtight container for up to 3 days.

Nutrition per serving
energy 86 kcals, fat 3g, saturates 0.3g, carbs 13g, sugars 4g, fibre 2g, protein 2g, salt 0.04g

Malty choc chip cookies

Try these easy, chewy chocolate chip cookies with malted milk – pop in the biscuit tin or cookie jar for up to 5 days.

 PREP 15 mins COOK 10 mins   MAKES 20

- 140g butter, softened
- 50g golden caster sugar
- 100g light brown soft sugar
- 2 medium eggs
- 200g plain flour
- 175g malted milk drink powder
- ½ tsp baking powder
- 100g dark chocolate, chopped

1 Heat the oven to 180C/160C fan/gas 4 and line two baking sheets with parchment. Beat the butter and sugars in a bowl until light and fluffy, then beat in the eggs one at a time.

2 Add the flour, malted milk drink powder, baking powder and a good pinch of salt, then stir with a wooden spoon until the mixture forms a dough. Tip out onto the work surface and gently knead in the chocolate. Divide the mixture into 20 pieces, roughly the size of a whole walnut. Roll each piece into a ball and place on the baking trays, leaving plenty of room for the cookies to spread. Flatten each ball slightly with your hand.

3 Bake for 10–12 mins until starting to turn golden brown on the edges. Remove from the oven, leave on the baking tray for 5 mins to cool slightly then transfer to a rack to cool completely. Will keep in a cake tin or cookie jar for up to 5 days.

Nutrition per serving
energy 186 kcals, fat 9g, saturates 5g, carbs 24g, sugars 14g, fibre 1g, protein 3g, salt 0.3g

Chocolate hazelnut thumbprint cookies

The food processor does most of the work in this recipe. The thumbprinting is an effective design, and means you can load plenty of chocolate into them.

 PREP 20 mins + chilling COOK 20 mins   MAKES 25

- 180g hazelnuts, toasted
- 100g plain flour
- 90g buckwheat flour
- 60g golden caster sugar
- 180g unsalted butter
- 100g dark chocolate, roughly chopped
- 1 tsp coconut oil (or use any flavourless oil)

1 Line a baking tray with parchment. Tip the hazelnuts into the bowl of a food processor and pulse until finely chopped. Add the flours, sugar and a pinch of flaked sea salt, and process for 20–30 secs until fully combined. Add the butter and pulse until the mixture just starts to come together. Tip the dough out onto a work surface and knead by hand until smooth.

2 Roll the dough into 25 small balls, then transfer to the prepared baking tray. Using your thumb or the handle of a wooden spoon, make an indent in the centre of each piece of dough. Put the tray in the fridge and chill for 30 mins before baking. Heat the oven to 180C/160C fan/gas 4.

3 Bake in the oven for 15–20 mins or until light golden brown. Put the chocolate and oil in a heatproof bowl and set over a pan of simmering water, stirring occasionally, until fully melted. Use a teaspoon to top each cookie with a little melted chocolate. Put aside until the chocolate has set.

Nutrition per serving
energy 163 kcals, fat 12g, saturates 5g, carbs 9g, sugars 4g, fibre 1g, protein 2g, salt 0g

Chapter 3

CELEBRATION BISCUITS

. . . .

There's always an occasion to bake a biscuit. Whether that's Christmas, when everyone reaches for gingerbread and cookies, Valentine's Day, Halloween or even the New Year, there's a biscuit for each celebration. Celebrate in style by baking these decorated biscuits, which are perfect for parties and make the ultimate presents.

Biscuit place tags

Make these little name biscuits as a fun addition to your party table for a celebration – one for each guest. They also make thoughtful gifts for family and friends.

 PREP 50 mins + chilling + setting COOK 15 mins   MAKES 10–12

- 100g butter
- 60g caster sugar
- 160g plain flour plus extra for dusting
- 1 tsp ground cinnamon
- ¼–½ tsp ground cardamom
- 1 egg yolk
- 1 tsp vanilla extract
- 100g royal icing sugar
- few drops of food colouring (optional)

YOU WILL NEED

- your choice of 8–10cm cookie cutters

1 Put the butter, sugar, flour and spices in a food processor and pulse until the mixture resembles breadcrumbs. Add the yolk and vanilla and pulse again until it forms a dough. Will keep, wrapped, in the fridge for 3 days or the freezer for 3 months.

2 Roll the dough out on a dusted work surface to the thickness of a £1 coin. Use cutters in the shapes of your choice to stamp out the tags, making sure they're large enough to pipe names on (we used round- and star-shaped cutters). Transfer the biscuits, well-spaced, to baking sheets lined with parchment and chill for 15 mins.

3 Heat the oven to 180C/160C fan/gas 4. Bake for 12–15 mins until golden at the edges. Cool for 5 mins on the sheets, then transfer to a rack.

4 Mix the icing sugar with 2–3 tsp water to make a very thick, stiff paste. Colour the icing with food colouring if you like. Transfer to a piping bag fitted with a very small round nozzle, and pipe borders around the biscuits, then the names in the centre. Leave to set for 2–3 hrs.

Nutrition per serving
energy 171 kcals, fat 8g, saturates 5g, carbs 24g, sugars 13g, fibre 1g, protein 2g, salt 0.2g

Valentine's biscuits

● ●

These picture-perfect sweet treats make a gorgeous gift for someone special. Create dough cylinders then simply slice and bake the number of biscuits you want.

 PREP 30 mins + freezing + chilling COOK 20 mins   MAKES 16-20

- 300g plain flour, plus a little extra for dusting
- 200g salted butter, diced
- 120g golden caster sugar
- 2 large egg yolks
- 2 tsp vanilla extract
- ½ tsp rosewater or 25g freeze-dried raspberries, whizzed to a powder (optional)
- red or pink food colouring

YOU WILL NEED
- 1 x 3-4cm heart-shaped cookie cutter

1 Whizz the flour and butter to fine crumbs in a processor. Add the sugar and yolks and mix to form a dough. Remove one-third, add vanilla to what's left and pulse. Wrap in cling film and leave at room temperature.

2 Put the plain dough in the processor with the rosewater and pulse, adding enough colour for an intense red. If the dough softens, pulse in flour. Chill. Remove 30 mins before rolling.

3 Between parchment, thickly roll out the red dough. Use a cutter to stamp out hearts, line up on top of each other and press into a cylinder, retaining the shape. Wrap in cling film and freeze for 3 hrs until solid.

4 Roll the vanilla dough with your hands into three cylinders the length of the hearts. Stick one to each 'side' of the frozen hearts, pat together to form a fat cylinder, then roll until it encircles the coloured dough. Chill for 2 hrs.

5 Heat the oven to 180C/160C fan/gas 4. Slice the log into 1cm discs. Place on lined trays, allowing space, and bake for 20 mins. Cool on racks. Keeps for 4 days in an airtight tin.

● ●

Nutrition per serving
energy 159 kcals, fat 9g, saturates 5g, carbs 17g, sugars 6g, fibre 1g, protein 2g, salt 0.2g

Easy Easter biscuits

Celebrate Easter and the start of spring with these easy currant biscuits flavoured with lemon and nutmeg.

 PREP 30 mins + chilling COOK 15 mins   MAKES 40

- 250g unsalted butter, softened
- 140g golden caster sugar, plus extra for sprinkling
- 1 medium egg, separated and beaten
- 1 lemon, zested
- generous grating of nutmeg
- 300g plain flour, plus extra for dusting
- ½ tsp fine salt
- 60g currants

YOU WILL NEED
- 1 x 6cm fluted biscuit cutter

1 Heat the oven to 180C/160 fan/gas 4. Place the butter and sugar in a bowl and beat with a wooden spoon until combined. Add the egg yolk, zest and nutmeg and beat again.
2 Add the flour, salt and currants and mix everything together to make a firm dough, using your hands if necessary. Form into a puck-shape, wrap and chill for 30 mins.
3 Line two large baking sheets with parchment and lightly dust your work surface with flour. Cut the dough in half and roll out to a ½ cm thickness. Cut out biscuits using a cutter, lift onto one of the baking sheets with a palette knife, leaving a little space in between. Repeat with the remaining pastry to make a second tray of biscuits, re-rolling the off-cuts. Chill for 30 mins.
4 Bake for 7 mins, then remove from the oven, brush with egg white, sprinkle with extra sugar and return for 7–8 mins until lightly golden brown. Cool on the trays for 5 mins then carefully transfer to a rack to cool completely.

Nutrition per serving
energy 100 kcals, fat 5g, saturates 3g, carbs 12g, sugars 6g, fibre 0.4g, protein 1g, salt 0.07g

White rabbit biscuits

• •

These adorable bunny biscuits will hop off the plate faster than you can bake them.
They make a great Easter activity for kids or an extra-special gift.

 PREP 1 hr 10 mins COOK 15 mins    MAKES 23–26 biscuits or 12 bunnies

• 1 x Basic biscuit dough
  (see page 10)

FOR THE ICING
• 450g icing sugar
• pink food colouring gel
• 125g desiccated coconut
• 12 mini marshmallows

YOU WILL NEED
• 1 x rabbit head-shaped
  cookie cutter
• 1 x 7cm round cookie cutter
• 1 x 3cm round cookie cutter

1 Heat the oven to 180C/160C fan/gas 4. Roll
   the dough out on a lightly floured surface
   until ½ cm thick. Cut into shapes. We did
   12 rabbit heads, 12 circles and 24 mini circles
2 Place on baking sheets lined with parchment
   and bake for 15 mins till golden at the edges.
   Cool for a few mins, then transfer to a rack.
3 Mix enough cold water with the icing sugar t
   create a thick icing. Place a quarter in a bow
   and add a tiny amount of pink gel. Transfer
   both icings into disposable piping bags and
   snip off the ends to make a very small nozzle
   on the pink and a wider one on the white.
4 Pipe white icing over the small biscuits and
   dry. Cover all the other biscuits with white
   icing (be sparing and it doesn't have to be
   neat). Sprinkle with coconut before they dry.
5 Create paws on the smaller circles with pink
   icing, then stick onto the large circles using
   icing like glue. Coat the marshmallows with
   icing and cover in coconut before sticking
   onto the middle of the larger circles to create
   a fluffy tail. Leave to set for 15–20 mins.

• •

Nutrition per serving
energy 467 kcals, fat 18g, saturates 12g, carbs 71g, sugars 51g, fibre 3g, protein 4g, salt 0.27g

Easter biscuit lollies

Make these cookies as gifts for friends or use them as place names on a celebratory dinner table.

 PREP 1 hr + chilling COOK 20 mins   MAKES 15

- 140g butter
- 100g light brown soft sugar
- 3 tbsp golden syrup
- ½ tsp vanilla extract
- 350g plain flour, plus extra for dusting
- 1 tsp bicarbonate of soda
- 1 large egg

FOR THE ICING
- food colouring
- 1kg pack ready-to-roll icing
- icing sugar, for dusting
- icing writing pens (we used white)

YOU WILL NEED
- 1 x egg-shaped cookie cutter

1 Heat the oven to 200C/180C fan/gas 6. Line two baking trays with parchment. Melt the butter, sugar and syrup, mix in the vanilla, remove from the heat and cool for 10 mins.
2 Sieve the flour and bicarb into a bowl. Pour in the butter mixture, add the egg and stir to form a stiff-ish dough. Chill for 10 mins to firm up. Roll out the dough on a floured surface to ½ cm thick and use a cutter to stamp out 15 egg shapes, re-rolling the dough. Poke a lollipop stick or coffee stirrer into the bottom of each, then bake for 12 mins until golden.
3 Knead food colouring into lumps of fondant icing. Roll out on a surface lightly dusted with icing sugar, then use the cutter to cut out egg shapes. Use the icing pens to dot a little icing on each biscuit, then stick on an icing shape.
4 Decorate the biscuits with the icing or pipe on names if you're planning to use them as place names for Easter lunch. Let them dry, then wrap in cellophane and tie with ribbons if you're giving them as gifts.

Nutrition per serving
energy 418 kcals. fat 8g. saturates 5g. carbs 82g. sugars 66g. fibre 1g. protein 3g. salt 0.4g

Hot cross cookies

Bored of buns? Try these cute cookies instead – sure to become a family favourite during Easter.

 PREP 20 mins COOK 10 mins MAKES 12

- 200g softened butter, plus extra for the trays
- 100g light muscovado sugar
- 1 egg
- 250g plain flour
- 1 tsp cinnamon
- 2 tsp baking powder
- 100g sultanas
- 200g white chocolate chips

1 Heat the oven to 180C/160C fan/gas 4. Lightly butter a few baking trays. In a large bowl, beat together the butter, sugar and egg until smooth. Sift in the flour, cinnamon and baking powder, then combine to make a dough. Add the sultanas and 100g of the white chocolate, and mix to combine.

2 Roll lumps of dough into balls the size of golf balls. Flatten these onto the trays, leaving enough space between each for them to expand. Bake for 10 mins until golden (you may have to do this in batches). Remove the cookies from the trays and cool on racks.

3 Melt the remaining white chocolate in the microwave. Using a small piping bag or a teaspoon, carefully drizzle a cross on top of each cookie. Leave to set before eating. These cookies can be stored in a cookie jar for up to 3 days.

Nutrition per serving
energy 231 kcals, fat 13g, saturates 8g, carbs 25g, sugars 16g, fibre 1g, protein 3g, salt 0.4g

Easter egg cookies

Create the perfect cookie with a soft, chewy centre and crisp outer edge. Mini eggs, white and dark chocolate chunks make them an indulgent Easter treat.

 PREP 20 mins COOK 35 mins   MAKES 20

- 175g butter, softened
- 200g light brown soft sugar
- 100g golden caster sugar
- 1 tbsp vanilla extract
- 1 large egg
- 250g plain flour
- ½ tsp bicarbonate of soda
- 50g white chocolate, chopped into chunks
- 100g bar dark chocolate, chopped into chunks
- 100g mini chocolate eggs, lightly crushed with a rolling pin, leaving some larger pieces to decorate

1 Heat the oven to 190C/170C fan/gas 5. Line two baking sheets with parchment. Tip the butter, sugars and vanilla into a bowl. Beat with a hand-held electric whisk until pale an fluffy. Add the egg and beat again. Tip in the flour, bicarb and a pinch of salt, then use a spatula to mix together before adding the chocolate and half the crushed mini eggs (set aside the larger pieces).

2 Scoop golf-ball-sized mounds of dough onto the baking sheets, leaving space. (You should fit four to six cookies on each, so you'll have to bake in batches.) Push the remaining mini egg pieces into the tops. Bake for 15–18 mins and swap the sheets halfway. For soft and chewy cookies, they should have golden edges but still be pale and soft in the middle. If you prefer a biscuit texture, bake for longer.

3 Remove from the oven and cool for 10 mins before transferring to a rack, then bake the second batch. Continue until all the cookies are baked. Will keep in an airtight container for up to a week.

Nutrition per serving
energy 241 kcals, fat 11g, saturates 7g, carbs 31g, sugars 21g, fibre 1g, protein 2g, salt 0.3g

Spider biscuits

Create these cute spider biscuits with kids as part of a Halloween party feast. Children will love adding the spooky chocolate spider legs and icing eyes.

 PREP 25 mins + cooling + setting   COOK 12 mins   MAKES 20

- 70g butter, softened
- 50g peanut butter
- 150g golden caster sugar
- 1 medium egg
- 1 tsp vanilla extract
- 180g plain flour
- ½ tsp bicarbonate of soda
- 20 peanut butter or chocolate caramel cups or chocolate honeycomb balls
- 100g milk chocolate, chopped
- icing eyes, or make your own

1 Heat the oven to 180C/160C fan/gas 4 and line two baking sheets with parchment. Using an electric hand whisk, cream the butter, peanut butter and sugar until light and fluffy, then beat in the egg and vanilla. Once combined, stir in the flour, bicarb and ¼ tsp salt.

2 Scoop 18–20 tbsp of the mixture onto the trays, leaving enough space between each to allow for spreading. Make a thumbprint in the centre of the cookies. Bake for 10–12 mins or until firm at the edges but still soft in the middle – they'll harden a little as they cool. Leave to cool on the tray for a few mins, then top with a peanut butter or caramel cup or honeycomb ball. Cool on a rack.

3 Heat the chocolate in the microwave or in a bowl set over a pan of simmering water. Scrape into a piping bag and leave to cool a little. Pipe the legs onto each spider, then stick two eyes on each. Leave to set. Will keep for 3 days in an airtight container.

Nutrition per serving
energy 161 kcals, fat 7g, saturates 4g, carbs 21g, sugars 13g, fibre 1g, protein 2g, salt 0.2g

White chocolate fortune cookies

Bake these fortune cookies for New Year's Eve. While they require a bit of effort, they keep keen cooks in the family entertained, and the results are seriously impressive.

 PREP 15 mins + chilling COOK 8 mins per batch   SERVES 4-6

- 2 egg whites
- 1 tsp vanilla extract
- 3 tbsp grapeseed oil
- 100g plain flour
- 2 tsp cornflour
- 100g golden caster sugar
- 150g white chocolate, chopped
- sprinkles, to decorate

1 Heat the oven to 180C/160C fan/gas 4. Line large baking sheet with silicone baking shee Write fortunes on 6cm x 1cm pieces of pape

2 Using an electric whisk, whisk the eggs, vanill and oil with ½ tbsp cold water for 30 second. until frothy. Sift the flour, cornflour, sugar and a good pinch of salt into the egg whites. Whisk to a smooth batter and chill for 1 hr.

3 Put ½ tbsp mixture on the sheet and use a palette knife to push out into an 8cm circle. Repeat to make two cookies. Bake two at a time for 8 mins until the edges are golden.

4 Use a palette knife to lift onto a board, flippin them over. Put a fortune in the middle, then fold in half, pinching to seal. Lift onto the rim of a mug/pan and pull the two corners dowr to shape. Hold for 10 seconds, then transfer t muffin tins to hold the shape. Repeat.

5 Melt the chocolate in the microwave or in a bowl set over a pan of simmering water. Dip in the ends of each cookie, then dip in the sprinkles. Leave to dry on a board. Keep for 3 days in an airtight container.

Nutrition per serving
energy 322 kcals, fat 14g, saturates 5g, carbs 45g, sugars 31g, fibre 1g, protein 5g, salt 0.1g

Your best year yet

Snowmen biscuits

. . . .

These snowmen biscuits are the perfect thing to bake during the festive season.
You can bake and freeze the biscuits ahead, then bring them out for a winter's day
activity.

 PREP 1 hr + cooling + setting COOK 14 mins   MAKES 24

- 1 x Basic biscuit dough
  (see page 10)

FOR THE DECORATION
- 480g white fondant icing
- icing sugar, for dusting
- 120g pack mixed red, yellow,
  black and blue ready-to-roll
  icing
- tube white icing, for sticking
- tube black icing

YOU WILL NEED
- 1 x 7cm round cookie cutter

1 Heat the oven to 190C/170C fan/gas 5. On a
   lightly floured surface, roll the dough to ½ cm
   then use a cutter to stamp out rounds.
2 Transfer to two baking trays lined with
   parchment and bake for 8–14 mins until the
   edges turn lightly golden. Leave to cool.
3 Roll out the fondant icing on a surface duste
   with icing sugar. Stamp out circles, then use
   white tube icing to stick on the biscuits.
4 Knead together yellow and blue icing to
   make green, then do the same with red and
   yellow to make orange. Roll out one colour c
   a time. Stamp out circles of coloured icing,
   cut in half and stick on for hats. Cut strips of
   another colour for hat bands, then stick on.
5 Decorate the hats with icing spots and stripe
   Roll out balls, poke holes with a cocktail stick
   and stick on as pom poms. Mould lumpy ball
   of orange for noses and black icing for eyes.
   Press to flatten, then stick on with white icing.
   Use the tube of black icing to pipe rows of
   dots for the smiles. Leave to set. Will keep for
   up to 5 days in an airtight container.

. . . .

Nutrition per serving
energy 213 kcals, fat 6g, saturates 4g, carbs 38g, sugars 28g, fibre 0.45g, protein 2g, salt 0.15g

Snowy owl Christmas tree biscuits

These edible decorations, topped with white and dark chocolate and almond 'feathers' are the perfect way to celebrate the Christmas season and make ornaments at home.

 PREP 1 hr COOK 14 mins   MAKES 6 large, 6 medium and 10 small owls

- 1 x Basic biscuit dough (see page 10)

FOR THE DECORATION

- 120g packet of whole blanched almonds
- 126g packet of giant white chocolate buttons
- 24g packet of standard-sized white chocolate buttons
- 60g dark chocolate chips
- 120g packet of flaked almonds, toasted
- gold edible glitter (optional)
- icing sugar, for dusting

YOU WILL NEED

- 1 x oval cookie cutter or cardboard template
- paintbrush
- fine string or ribbon, for hanging the biscuits

1 Heat the oven to 190C/170C fan/gas 5. Roll the dough out on a lightly floured surface to 5mm thick. Cut out ovals with a cutter or template.

2 Transfer to a baking tray lined with parchment. Push in the almonds to create eyebrows and beaks. Make a hole near the top using the end of a paintbrush. Bake for 8–14 minutes until the edges are light golden. Cool on the tray.

3 Set aside buttons to create the eyes (use giant or standard buttons depending on the size of the owls – the biggest you can fit are best). Melt the remainder in the microwave or in a bowl over barely simmering water.

4 Using a small tipped paintbrush, paint and stick down the decorations. Stick on the white buttons, then the choc chips on top to make the eyes. Paint more chocolate over each chest, pressing on the flaked almonds. Layer the almonds with extra white chocolate.

5 If any of the eyebrows or beaks have come loose, use chocolate to stick them. Leave to set. Thread the decorations with string or ribbon. Dust with gold glitter and icing sugar.

Nutrition per serving
energy 254 kcals, fat 15g, saturates 6g, carbs 24g, sugars 13g, fibre 1g, protein 5g, salt 0.16g

Lusikkaleivät (Finnish spoon biscuits)

Bake these delicate jam-filled biscuits at Christmas. They're a Finnish festive tradition, and the secret to their delicious nutty flavour is the brown butter.

 PREP 1 hr 15 mins + cooling COOK 12 mins   MAKES 30

- 200g unsalted butter
- 125g caster sugar
- 2 tsp vanilla sugar or 1 tsp vanilla paste
- 300g plain flour
- 1 tsp bicarbonate of soda

FOR THE FILLING

- 75g good-quality or homemade raspberry jam
- 50g caster sugar

1 Heat the oven to 195C/175C fan/gas 5½ and line two baking sheets with parchment.

2 Melt the butter in a pan over a low heat and cook for 10 mins, stirring regularly, until it turns golden and smells slightly nutty. Keep an eye on the colour as the butter can burn quickly. Immediately pour the butter into a large bowl, add the sugar and vanilla, and mix thoroughly. Leave to cool a little, then sieve in the flour and bicarb.

3 Use a large teaspoon to scoop pieces of the mixture and mould them, pushing down slightly to flatten the tops and smoothing away the excess on the sides with a finger. Slide off the spoon and arrange on the prepared baking sheets, flat side down. Repeat with the remaining mixture. Bake for 10–12 mins until light golden. Leave to cool completely.

4 Spread a small amount of jam on the flat side of each biscuit. Sandwich with another biscuit. Tip the sugar onto a plate, then roll each of the biscuits in it to coat.

Nutrition per serving
energy 117 kcals, fat 6g, saturates 4g, carbs 15g, sugars 8g, fibre 0.4g, protein 1g, salt 0.1g

Peppermint candy biscuits

These heart-shaped cookies with a crunchy mint filling are fun to make and give as present and the perfect way to use up your leftover candy canes.

 PREP 25 mins + chilling COOK 12 mins   MAKES about 20

- 175g plain flour, plus a little extra for dusting
- 100g butter, cut into small cubes
- 85g caster sugar
- 1 egg yolk
- about 5 peppermint candy canes

YOU WILL NEED
- 1 x large heart-shaped cookie cutter
- 1 x small heart-shaped cookie cutter

1 Tip the flour and butter into a bowl. Use your fingers to squash the butter into the flour, the rub together until it resembles wet sand. Add the sugar, yolk and 1–2 tbsp cold water. Mix with a cutlery knife, then hands, into a soft dough. Wrap in cling film and chill for 20 min

2 Heat the oven to 200C/180C fan/gas 6. Line two baking trays with parchment. Put the candy canes in a resealable plastic bag, then wrap in a tea towel. Use a rolling pin to bash to a chunky rubble. Set to one side.

3 Dust your work surface with flour, then roll ou the dough. Cut out heart shapes with the big cutter. Put on the trays, spaced apart. Use th small cutter to cut a little heart in the centres Re-roll the cuttings to make about 20 hearts.

4 Bake for 8 mins. Remove from the oven, then fill each heart with crushed candy cane. Return to the oven for 4 mins, until just starting to turn golden and the candy has melted.

5 Once out of the oven, quickly sprinkle the centres with extra crushed candy cane. Coo completely on the trays.

Nutrition per serving
energy 99 kcals, fat 5g, saturates 3g, carbs 14g, sugars 7g, fibre 0g, protein 1g, salt 0.1g

Christmas crinkle cookies

Love crinkle cookies? Try this extra-festive version for Christmas, with orange zest, mixed spice and cinnamon – and not forgetting the classic fudgy centre.

 PREP 20 mins + chilling COOK 10 mins   MAKES 30

- 60g cocoa powder, sieved
- 200g caster sugar
- 60ml vegetable oil
- 2 large eggs
- 180g plain flour
- 1 tsp baking powder
- 2 oranges, zested
- 2 tsp mixed spice
- 1 tsp cinnamon
- 50g icing sugar

1 Mix the cocoa, caster sugar and oil togethe Add the eggs one at a time, whisking until fully combined.

2 Combine the flour, baking powder, orange zest, mixed spice, cinnamon and a pinch of salt in a separate bowl, then add to the cocoa mixture and mix until a soft dough forms. If it feels too soft, put in the fridge to chill for 1 hr.

3 Heat the oven to 190C/170C fan/gas 5 and ti the icing sugar into a shallow dish. Roll heaped teaspoons of the dough into balls (about 20g each), then roll in the icing sugar to coat. Put the balls on one large or two medium baking trays lined with parchment, ensuring they're evenly spaced apart.

4 Bake on the middle rack of the oven for 10 mins, then transfer to a rack to cool – they will firm up as they cool, but still be fudgy in the centre. Will keep for up to 4 days in an airtight container.

Nutrition per serving
energy 88 kcals, fat 3g, saturates 1g, carbs 13g, sugars 8g, fibre 1g, protein 2g, salt 0.06g

Lebkuchen

A German biscuit similar to gingerbread, lebkuchen is easy to make and a great Christmas treat.

 PREP 15 mins COOK 15 mins  MAKES 30

- 250g plain flour
- 85g ground almond
- 2 tsp ground ginger
- 1 tsp ground cinnamon
- ½ tsp bicarbonate of soda
- 200ml clear honey
- 85g butter
- 1 lemon, finely grated zest
- pinch each ground cloves, grated nutmeg and black pepper
- 1 tsp baking powder

FOR THE ICING
- 100g icing sugar
- 1 egg white, beaten

1 Tip the dry ingredients into a large bowl. Heat the honey and butter in a pan over a low heat until the butter melts, then pour into the flour mixture along with the lemon zest. Mix well until the dough is combined and fairly solid. Cover and leave to cool.

2 Heat the oven to 180C/160C fan/gas 4. Using your hands, roll the dough into about 30 balls, each 3cm wide, then flatten each one slightly into a disc. Divide the biscuits between two baking trays lined with parchment, leaving room for them to expand. Bake for 15 mins, then cool on a rack.

3 To ice the biscuits, mix together the icing sugar, egg white and 1–2 tbsp water to form a smooth runny icing. Dip the top of each biscuit in the icing and spread with the back of a knife. Leave to dry out in a warm room.

Nutrition per serving
energy 102 kcals, fat 4g, saturates 2g, carbs 16g, sugars 9g, fibre 0.5g, protein 2g, salt 0.16g

Snowball biscuits

Get the kids to help roll the dough into its snowball-like shape to make these Christmas biscuits. Nutty and zesty, they're sure to be a family favourite.

 PREP:10 mins COOK:15 mins SERVES 10

- 100g pecans
- 70g plain flour
- 50g softened butter
- 25g caster sugar
- 1 orange, zested
- 2 tbsp icing sugar, plus extra for dusting

1 Heat the oven to 180C/160C fan/gas 4. Line a large baking tray with parchment. Tip the pecans into a food processor and blitz until they resemble a rough powder. Tip into a bowl and stir in the flour.

2 In a separate bowl, beat the butter, caster sugar and orange zest together with an electric whisk until pale and fluffy. Add the flour and pecan mix and stir with a wooden spoon until everything comes together in a rough dough. Shape into 10 even-sized balls and put on the tray.

3 Bake for 15 mins until set but the top is still pale in colour. Leave to cool on the tray for 5 mins, then, once cool enough to handle, gently roll the balls in the icing sugar and return to the tray. Leave to cool completely. Will keep in an airtight container for up to 5 days. Dust with more icing sugar just before serving.

Nutrition per serving
energy 258 kcals, fat 11g, saturates 3g, carbs 12g, sugars 6g, fibre 1g, protein 2g, salt 0.9g

Ultimate easy gingerbread

Make some gingerbread stars to hang from your Christmas tree. This biscuit dough is extremely forgiving if overworked, so it's perfect for baking with children.

 PREP 20 mins + chilling COOK 15 mins   SERVES 10

- 100g salted butter
- 3 tbsp golden syrup
- 100g dark muscovado sugar
- ½ tsp bicarbonate of soda
- 1 tbsp ground ginger
- 1 tsp ground cinnamon
- 225g plain flour
- 50g icing sugar

YOU WILL NEED
- 1 x 9cm star-shaped cookie cutter or any shape cutter
- piping bag with a thin nozzle
- fine string or ribbon, for hanging

1 Heat the butter, syrup and sugar in a pan until melted, stirring occasionally. Cool slightly.
2 Mix the bicarb, ginger, cinnamon and flour together. Pour in the syrup mixture and stir, then use your hands to bring together into a soft dough.
3 Put the dough on a sheet of parchment, shape into a rectangle, then lay another sheet on top. Roll out to a thickness of 5mm. Transfer to a baking sheet to keep it flat, leaving the parchment in place. Chill for 1 h
4 Heat the oven to 190C/170C fan/gas 5 and line a large baking sheet with parchment. C out star shapes, making some with stars cut out to thread ribbon through for hanging.
5 Place the shapes, spread apart, on the shee and bake for 10–12 mins. Depending on size, they might need a few minutes more or less. Leave to cool completely.
6 Mix the icing sugar with 1–2 tbsp water – you want a thick and pipeable consistency. Pipe the icing over the cooled biscuits.

Nutrition per serving
energy 150 kcals, fat 5g, saturates 3g, carbs 23g, sugars 12g, fibre 1g, protein 2g, salt 0.2g

Chapter 4

ICED BISCUITS

. . . .

In our opinion, there's nothing more cathartic than taking time to decorate beautiful biscuits that look like a work of art but are surprisingly easy to do. From simple iced biscuits to more challenging fancy cookies, you can work your way through the recipes, learning new skills through each design.

Simple iced biscuits

Make these sweet iced letters and numbers. This is the perfect basic recipe for any beginner bakers or those who love to keep it simple and classic.

 PREP 30 mins COOK 20 mins   MAKES 30–35

- 1 x Basic biscuit dough (see page 10)

TO DECORATE
- 8–10 x 19g coloured icing pens, or fondant icing sugar mixed with a little water and food colouring

YOU WILL NEED
- letter and number cookie cutters (we used 7 x 4cm)

1 Heat the oven to 200C/180C fan/gas 6.
2 Cut the dough into six pieces and roll out or at a time to about a 5mm thickness on a floured surface. The easiest way to do this is roll the mixture out on a baking mat. Cut ou letter and number shapes and peel away th leftover dough at the edges. Re-roll any off-cuts and repeat.
3 Transfer the whole mat or the individual biscuits to two baking sheets (transfer them parchment if not using a mat) and bake for 7–10 mins or until the edges are just brown. Leave to cool completely and repeat with the rest of the dough. You should be able to fit about 12 on each sheet. If you are using two sheets, then the one underneath will tak a minute longer.
4 Ice the biscuits using the pens to make stripe or dots, or colour in the whole biscuit if you like. They will keep for up to 5 days in an airtight container.

Nutrition per serving
energy 89 kcals, fat 4g, saturates 2g, carbs 12g, sugars 4g, fibre 0.3g, protein 1g, salt 0.09g

Honeybread biscuits

These decorative biscuits are the perfect gift to include in a summertime hamper or give to guests with a cup of tea.

 PREP 1 hour COOK 12 mins MAKES 22

- 300g plain flour
- 100g diced butter
- 1 tbsp mixed spice
- 2 tsp ground ginger
- 100g light brown soft sugar
- 1 large egg
- 100g clear honey

TO DECORATE
- runny white icing
- granulated or caster sugar
- black and yellow coloured icing pens, or fondant icing sugar mixed with a little water and food colouring

YOU WILL NEED
- 1 x honey bee-shaped cookie cutter or a cardboard template

1 Put the flour, butter, mixed spice, ginger, sugar, egg and honey in a food processor. Whizz to a smooth dough.
2 Roll out the dough on a lightly flour-dusted surface to a £1 coin thickness, then stamp o honey bee shapes. Bake on baking trays at 200C/180C fan/gas 6 for 10–12 mins until cris and golden brown.
3 After baking, brush the wings with a little runny icing, then dip into the granulated or caster sugar to coat. Add black and yellow stripes with the icing pens.

Nutrition per serving
energy 120 kcals, fat 4g, saturates 3g, carbs 18g, sugars 8g, fibre 1g, protein 2g, salt 0.11g

Bunting biscuits

Add a touch of fun to your party with these edible flag-shaped cookies - ice in your favourite colours.

 PREP 50 mins COOK 10 mins   MAKES 22

- 350g plain flour, plus a little extra for rolling
- 100g cold butter, diced
- 1 tsp bicarbonate of soda
- 140g light brown soft sugar
- 1 large egg
- 75g golden syrup
- 2 tsp vanilla extract

TO DECORATE
- 1kg pack ready-to-roll icing
- few food colourings and coloured icing pens, in your favourite colours
- icing sugar

YOU WILL NEED
- 1 x triangle-shaped cardboard template
- string or ribbon, for hanging

1 Put the flour, butter, bicarb and sugar in a food processor, whizz until you can't see any lumps butter, then tip into a mixing bowl. Whisk the egg, syrup and vanilla together, then stir into the bowl with a wooden spoon. Knead togethe into a smooth dough.

2 Heat the oven to 200C/180C fan/gas 6. Roll ou the dough on a lightly floured surface and use the template to cut out triangles, re-rolling as you go. Line some baking sheets with parchment and lift on the biscuits. Use a penci end to make two holes in the top of each one – not too close to the edge. Bake, one tray at c time, for 8–10 mins, remaking each hole when the biscuits are just out and still soft. Cool.

3 Divide the icing and knead in your chosen foo colourings. Roll out thinly on a surface dusted with icing sugar and cut out more triangles. Brush the backs with water and stick onto the biscuits – making holes in the icing to match the biscuits. Decorate with icing pens and circles o icing, then thread through the string or ribbon.

Nutrition per serving
energy 258 kcals, fat 4g, saturates 2g, carbs 53g, sugars 44g, fibre 1g, protein 2g, salt 0.2g

Spiced acorn biscuits

Bake simple biscuits using a little acorn flour to add a hint of nuttiness and a slightly more robust texture.

 PREP 20 mins + chilling + setting COOK 10 mins   MAKES 24

- 200g unsalted butter, cubed
- 275–300g plain flour, plus extra for dusting
- 25–50g acorn flour
- 100g golden caster sugar
- 1 egg, plus 1 yolk
- ½ tsp vanilla extract
- 1 tsp mixed spice or cinnamon
- white icing or melted chocolate, to decorate

YOU WILL NEED

- squirrel and acorn-shaped cookie cutters, cardboard templates or any cutters

1 Rub the butter into the flours using your finger until the mixture resembles breadcrumbs, then stir in the sugar, the egg and yolk, vanilla, mixed spice or cinnamon and bring together to form a dough. Roll out on a light floured surface and stamp out biscuits in any shapes you like. Re-roll the trimmings and repeat. Arrange on parchment-lined trays and chill for 30 mins.

2 Heat the oven to 200C/180C fan/gas 6. Bake the biscuits for 10 mins, then leave to cool. Decorate with icing, or dip one side in chocolate and leave to set.

Nutrition per serving
energy 138 kcals, fat 8g, saturates 5g, carbs 14g, sugars 4g, fibre 1g, protein 2g, salt 0g

Caption biscuits

Ideal for celebrations, birthdays or any occasion, these hand-held iced and decorate biscuits are a sweet way to get your message across.

 PREP 10 mins + chilling + decorating COOK 12 mins   MAKES 24

FOR THE COOKIES
- 175g soft butter, plus extra for greasing
- 100g golden caster sugar
- 1 large egg yolk
- ½ tsp vanilla extract
- zest 1 lemon
- 250g plain flour, plus extra for rolling
- ½ tsp salt

TO DECORATE
- 200g icing sugar, sifted
- 1 large egg white
- food colourings of your choice, we used orange and pink

YOU WILL NEED
- 1 x 8cm round cookie cutter
- cake pops or lolly sticks
- piping bag

1 Beat the butter and sugar until pale and cream then beat in the yolk, vanilla and zest. Sift the flour and salt into the bowl, then stir in to make soft dough. Split into two flat discs, then wrap in cling film and chill for 30 mins, or until firm. Heat the oven to 180C/160C fan/gas 4. Line two baking sheets.

2 Flour the work surface, then roll the dough to the thickness of two £2 coins. Stamp out circles and re-roll the trimmings. Chill for 10 mins, then poke the sticks carefully into the dough.

3 Bake for 12 mins, until pale golden. Leave on the tray for 5 mins before transferring to a rack to cool. Make the icing by beating the sugar and egg white until thick and smooth. Remove half t another bowl, colour, then spoon into the piping bag and snip off the tip. Pipe a speech bubble border around each biscuit and leave to set.

4 Loosen the white icing with a few drops of water until runny. Spoon a little onto each biscuit and let it flood to the outline. Dry for 10 mins, then pipe captions on top. Leave to dry.

Nutrition per serving
energy 214 kcals, fat 8g, saturates 5g, carbs 34g, sugars 25g, fibre 1g, protein 2g, salt

Funny face biscuits

These fashionable moustache and retro lip biscuits are ideal as wedding favours or as part of a children's party buffet.

 PREP 10 mins + chilling + decorating COOK 24 mins   MAKES about 24

- 1 x Basic biscuit dough (see page 10)

TO DECORATE
- 1 large egg white
- 200g icing sugar
- pink and brown food colouring pastes
- pink and gold edible glitter (optional)

YOU WILL NEED
- 1 x 8cm round cookie cutter
- cake pops or lolly sticks
- 2 x piping bags

1 Heat the oven to 180C/160C fan/gas 4.
2 Roll the dough to a 5mm thickness on a floured surface. Stamp out circles and cut a crescent moon and a pointy oval shape from each. Pinch each oval's corners and indent the top and bottom to make lips. Shape the moons into moustaches by pressing a dent into the top of the curve, tweaking the ends.
3 Chill for 10 mins, then poke in the sticks. Bake on two lined baking sheets for 12 mins, one tray at a time, until pale golden. Leave for 5 mins before sliding onto a rack to cool. Beat the egg white and sugar to a thick, smooth icing. Divide into four and colour with two shades of pink and two of brown. Fill the bags with the darker icings and snip off the tips.
5 Pipe moustache and lip outlines and dry for a few mins. Loosen the paler icings with a few drops of water until runny. Spoon onto each biscuit and let it flood to the outline. Dry for 10 mins, then pipe a darker mouth line onto the lips and zig-zag lines over the moustaches. Sprinkle with glitter and leave to set.

Nutrition per serving
energy 156 kcals, fat 6g, saturates 3g, carbs 24g, sugars 15g, fibre 1g, protein 2g, salt 0.14g

Love bug biscuits

These cute cookies decorated with fondant icing in a heart-shaped ladybird pattern would make a lovely romantic gift.

 PREP 30 mins + chilling COOK 12 mins   MAKES 20

- 175g plain flour
- 100g chilled butter, cubed
- 85g icing sugar
- 1 tsp vanilla extract
- 1 egg yolk

TO DECORATE
- 500g ready-to-roll fondant icing
- red food colouring
- 100g icing sugar
- black food colouring
- edible pearly ball decorations

YOU WILL NEED
- 1 x 8cm heart-shaped cookie cutter
- 1 x 6cm heart-shaped cookie cutter
- piping bag with a small plain nozzle

1 Put the flour, butter, sugar, vanilla and egg yolk in a food processor. Dribble in 1 tbsp water and blitz until the mixture comes together to form a dough. Tip onto a work surface and knead briefly to bring together, then wrap in cling film and chill for 20 mins.

2 Heat the oven to 180C/160C fan/gas 4. Roll out the dough to the thickness of a £1 coin. Use your 8cm cutter to stamp out hearts, re-rolling as you go. Put the hearts on two baking trays and bake for 12 mins, swapping over halfway through, until pale golden. Leave to cool.

3 Dye your icing with red food colouring and wrap in cling film until ready to roll. Mix the icing sugar with enough water to make a thick icing, add black food colouring and pour into a piping bag. Roll out the red icing to 3mm thick and use your 6cm cutter to stamp out hearts. Stick onto the biscuits with some icing.

4 Decorate your love bugs with black icing and stick 2 pearly balls onto each love bug's head. Leave to set.

Nutrition per serving
energy 166 kcals, fat 5g, saturates 3g, carbs 29g, sugars 22g, fibre 0g, protein 1g, salt 0.1g

Chapter 5

BAKE SALE BISCUITS

. . . .

Be the star of the bake sale table with these biscuit recipes.
There are lots of simple and easy recipes that are perfect for
making with little helpers, along with beautiful biscuits that
will impress anyone who sees them!

Snickerdoodles

Is your dream biscuit crisp on the outside and soft in the middle? If so, these cinnamon biscuits are for you. A classic American bake, they're popular for a reaso

 PREP 20 mins + cooling COOK 12 mins   MAKES 18

- 200g unsalted butter, softened
- 150g caster sugar
- 50g light brown soft sugar
- 2 tsp vanilla bean paste
- 300g plain flour
- 1½ tsp cream of tartar
- 1 tsp bicarbonate of soda
- 3 tbsp milk

FOR THE TOPPING
- 3 tbsp caster sugar
- 1 tbsp ground cinnamon

1 Heat the oven to 200C/180C fan/gas 6 and line two baking trays with parchment. Beat the butter and both sugars in a large bowl using an electric whisk for 2 mins until smoo and fluffy.

2 Add the vanilla and beat until combined, scraping down the sides once. Add the flou cream of tartar, bicarbonate of soda and ¼ tsp salt and mix until just combined. Stir in the milk to loosen the mixture.

3 For the topping, combine the sugar and cinnamon in a shallow bowl. Roll 40g of the dough into a ball. Roll the dough ball in the cinnamon-sugar mixture, then place it on a prepared tray and press it down lightly. Repeat with the remaining dough and topping, spacing the balls about 5cm apar

4 Bake for 10–12 mins until golden and puffed up. Leave to cool on the trays for 5 mins, the transfer to a rack to cool completely. Will keep in an airtight tin for up to 4 days.

Nutrition per serving
energy 205 kcals, fat 10g, saturates 6g, carbs 28g, sugars 15g, fibre 1g, protein 2g, salt 0.2g

Red velvet biscuits

Turn the popular cake into chewy biscuits, complete with cream cheese icing. They'r perfect to make ahead for a bake sale or make a batch of dough to keep in the freez

 PREP 20 mins + chilling COOK 15 mins   MAKES 16–18

- 175g soft salted butter
- 200g light brown soft sugar
- 100g caster sugar
- 1 large egg
- 2 tsp vanilla extract
- ½–1 tbsp red food colouring gel, depending on strength
- 225g plain flour
- 25g cocoa powder
- ½ tsp bicarbonate of soda
- 150g white chocolate chips or chunks

FOR THE DRIZZLE
- 2 tbsp soft cheese
- 6 tbsp icing sugar

YOU WILL NEED
- piping bag (optional)

1 Heat the oven to 190C/170C fan/gas 5. Beat the butter and sugars together with an elect whisk until pale and fluffy. Beat in the egg, vanilla and food colouring until you have a bright red batter. Sieve over the flour, cocoa and bicarb and fold in to make a stiff, evenly coloured dough, then fold in the choc chips

2 Put the dough on a sheet of parchment, fold the parchment over the dough and mould into a sausage shape 6cm wide. Cut the cookie dough into 1cm-thick slices and arrange on two large trays lined with parchment, well-spaced apart. Bake in batches, keeping the unbaked cookies in the fridge while the rest are baking.

4 Bake for 13–15 mins until the biscuits are crisp at the edges, but still soft in the centre. Leave to cool on the tray for a few minutes, then transfer to a rack to cool completely. Beat th soft cheese in a bowl to a loose consistency, then stir in the icing sugar. Use a piping bag o a spoon to drizzle the icing over the cookies.

Nutrition per serving
energy 268 kcals, fat 12g, saturates 7g, carbs 36g, sugars 26g, fibre 1g, protein 3g, salt 0.3g

Empire biscuits

Make a batch of these easy classic empire biscuits. Sandwich with raspberry jam and top with thick icing and a glacé cherry to finish.

 PREP 35 mins + chilling + setting COOK 12 mins   MAKES 12-14

- 175g plain flour, plus extra for dusting
- 100g cold salted butter, cut into cubes
- 335g icing sugar
- ½ tsp vanilla extract
- 2 medium egg yolks
- 100g raspberry jam
- 50g glacé cherries, quartered

YOU WILL NEED
- 1 x 7cm round cookie cutter
- piping bag (optional)

1 Put the flour, butter, 85g of the icing sugar, the vanilla and yolks in a food processor and pulse in bursts until combined (alternatively, rub together the butter and flour with your fingertips and mix in the sugar, vanilla and egg yolks). Add ½ tbsp water if the mix feels a little dry. Tip the rough mixture onto a work surface and briefly knead until the dough has come together. Wrap and chill for 30 mins.

2 Heat the oven to 180C/160C fan/gas 4. Line two baking sheets with parchment. Dust your work surface with flour and roll the dough out to 3mm thick. Cut about 24 rounds from the dough, then add to the baking sheets and bake for 10–12 mins until the edges are lightly golden. Transfer to a rack to cool completely.

3 Mix the remaining sugar with 2–3 tsp water to make a very thick icing. Spoon or pipe over half the biscuits, leaving a border. Top with a cherry, then set for 30 mins. Spread jam over the un-iced biscuits and sandwich with the iced. Will keep for 2 days in an airtight tin.

Nutrition per serving
energy 305 kcals, fat 7g, saturates 4g, carbs 59g, sugars 46g, fibre 1g, protein 2g, salt 0.15g

Brookies

Do you love both brownies and cookies, but struggle to choose between the two? We've combined them both in our brookie recipe, so you get the best of both worlds.

 PREP 20 mins + chilling and cooling COOK 30 mins   MAKES 16

FOR THE COOKIE LAYER

- 120g unsalted butter, softened
- 120g light brown soft sugar
- 100g dark muscovado sugar
- 1 large egg, plus 1 egg yolk
- 250g plain flour
- ½ tsp bicarbonate of soda
- 50g milk chocolate chunks

FOR THE BROWNIE LAYER

- 185g unsalted butter
- 185g dark chocolate (at least 70% cocoa solids)
- 3 large eggs
- 1 tsp vanilla extract
- 275g golden caster sugar
- 50g cocoa powder
- 130g plain flour
- 50g milk chocolate chunks

YOU WILL NEED

- 23cm square cake tin

1 Grease the tin and line with parchment. Heat the oven to 180C/160C fan/gas 4. First, make the cookie layer. Put the butter and both sugars in a bowl and beat with an electric whisk. Alternatively, do this in a stand mixer. Add the egg and yolk and beat. Mix in the flour, ¼ tsp salt, the bicarb and choc chunks. Press into the base of the tin. Chill for 30 mins.

2 For the brownie layer, melt the butter and chocolate in a heatproof bowl over a pan of simmering water, stirring until smooth. Cool for 10 mins. Whisk the eggs, vanilla and sugar in a bowl with an electric whisk for 3 mins until slightly thickened. Fold the cooled chocolate mixture through the eggs until well combined.

3 Fold the chocolate mix, cocoa and flour together. Spoon this brownie mixture over the cookie dough layer, dot with choc chunks and sprinkle with sea salt. Bake for 50 mins–1 hr or until a skewer inserted into the middle comes out with just a few crumbs clinging to it. Cool in the tin before cutting into squares.

Nutrition per serving
energy 489 kcals, fat 25g, saturates 15g, carbs 57g, sugars 37g, fibre 3g, protein 7g, salt 0.3g

Ginger fairings

Delicately spiced biscuits with a moreish crunch, these West Country snaps are perfect for fairs and bake sales.

 PREP 10 mins COOK 10 mins  MAKES 18

- 100g butter, diced, plus extra for the baking sheet
- 225g plain flour
- 2 tsp baking powder
- 2 tsp bicarbonate of soda
- 1 tbsp ground ginger
- 2 tsp mixed spice
- 100g caster sugar
- 4 tbsp golden syrup

1 Heat the oven to 200C/180C fan/gas 6. Lightly butter two large baking sheets. Put the flour, ¼ tsp salt, baking powder, bicarb and spices in a food processor. Add the butter and whizz until the mixture resembles breadcrumbs. Tip into a bowl and stir in the sugar.

2 Gently warm the golden syrup in a pan, add to the mixture and stir to form a dough. Roll the dough into 16 walnut-sized balls, then arrange, at least 2cm apart, on the baking sheets. Bake for 8–10 mins until golden. Cool on the trays before transferring to a rack.

Nutrition per serving
energy 136 kcals, fat 5g, saturates 3g, carbs 21g, sugars 10g, fibre 1g, protein 2g, salt 0.6g

Chocolate fudge crinkle biscuits

Use store cupboard ingredients to make these moreish chocolate fudge crinkle biscuits. They're quick and easy to make and a real crowd pleaser.

 PREP 20 mins + chilling COOK 10 mins   MAKES 35–40

- 60g cocoa powder, sieved
- 200g caster sugar
- 60ml vegetable oil
- 2 large eggs
- 180g plain flour
- 1 tsp baking powder
- 70g icing sugar

1 Mix the cocoa, caster sugar and oil together. Add the eggs one at a time, whisking until fully combined.
2 Stir the flour, baking powder and a pinch of salt together in a separate bowl, then add to the cocoa mixture and mix until a soft dough forms. If it feels soft, transfer to the fridge and chill for 1 hr.
3 Heat the oven to 190C/170C fan/gas 5. Tip the icing sugar into a shallow dish. Form a heaped teaspoon of the dough into a ball, then roll in the sugar to coat. Repeat with the rest of the dough, then put, evenly spaced, on a baking tray lined with parchment.
4 Bake in the centre of the oven for 10 mins – they will firm up as they cool. Transfer to a rack and leave to cool. Will keep for 4 days in a biscuit tin.

Nutrition per serving
energy 67 kcals, fat 2g, saturates 0.4g, carbs 10g, sugars 7g, fibre 0.4g, protein 1g, salt 0.04g

Double chocolate shortbreads

You're only five ingredients away from this double chocolate, melt-in-your-mouth shortbread delight.

 PREP 10 mins COOK 12 mins   MAKES 10

- 175g butter, softened
- 85g golden caster sugar
- 200g plain flour
- 2 tbsp cocoa powder
- 100g chocolate chips, milk or dark

1 Mix the butter and sugar together with a wooden spoon. Stir in the flour and cocoa, followed by the chocolate chips – you'll probably need to mix the dough together with your hands at this stage. Halve the dough and roll each piece into a log about 5cm across. Wrap and chill for 1 hr or up to several days. Can be frozen for up to 1 month.

2 Heat the oven to 180C/160C fan/gas 4. Slice logs into 1cm-thick rounds, transfer to a baking tray lined with parchment and bake for 10–12 mins. Cool on the tray.

Nutrition per serving
energy 290 kcals, fat 18g, saturates 11g, carbs 31g, sugars 15g, fibre 1g, protein 3g, salt 0.22g

Funfetti biscuits

Enjoy making these fun, bright and colourful funfetti biscuits with little ones as they're so quick and easy to do.

 PREP 30 mins + chilling COOK 10–20 mins   MAKES 32 biscuits or 120 bites

- 200g butter, softened
- 1 tsp vanilla extract
- 85g golden caster sugar
- 80g ground rice
- 225g plain flour
- 6 tbsp funfetti or sprinkles

1 Put the butter, vanilla and sugar in a large mixing bowl and stir with a wooden spoon until smooth. Add the ground rice, then stir in the flour and sprinkles. If the mixture starts to get dry, use your hands to bring everything together and make a smooth dough.

2 You can now choose between two different types of biscuit. If you want to make round ones, divide the dough in two. Lay out a piece of parchment or foil and shape the first lump of dough into a log, about 4–5cm across. Roll it up and chill for at least 30 mins. Repeat with the second piece of dough. If you want to make mini biscuits, roll out the dough on the parchment in a single layer about ½ cm thick. Wrap and chill as above.

3 Heat the oven to 180C/160C fan/gas 4. Either slice the logs into rounds about ½ cm thick, or cut the slab into small squares, about 3cm each side. Bake on lined baking sheets for 20 mins for the large biscuits or 10 mins for small ones, until lightly golden. Leave to cool for 5 mins on the baking sheets, then slide onto racks to cool completely.

Nutrition per serving
energy 107 kcals, fat 6g, saturates 4g, carbs 12g, sugars 5g, fibre 0.3g, protein 1g, salt 0.1g

Carrot cake biscuits

A universal favourite, in biscuit form! Give your standard carrot cake an upgrade with these bite-sized biscuity treats.

 PREP 30 mins + chilling COOK 20 mins   MAKES 14

- 140g cream cheese
- 140g icing sugar, plus 3 tbsp
- ½ tsp vanilla extract
- 350g plain flour, plus extra for dusting your hands
- ½ tsp baking powder
- 1 tsp ground cinnamon
- 1 tsp mixed spice
- 140g butter, softened
- 140g soft light brown sugar
- 1 egg beaten
- 200g carrot, finely grated
- zest and juice 1 orange
- 3 tbsp finely chopped walnuts

1 Mix together the cream cheese, 3 tbsp icing sugar and the vanilla extract in a bowl, then put in the freezer to firm up for 30 mins.

2 Mix the flour, baking powder and spices. In another bowl, beat the butter and sugar until creamy. Beat in the egg, then carrot. Tip in the dry ingredients and mix to form a dough.

3 Line a baking sheet with parchment. Dust your hands with flour, then divide the dough into 14 balls and place on the sheet. Use your palm to flatten to thin circles. Add 1 tsp of the cream cheese mix to the centres, then wrap the dough around the filling to seal, pinching the top and rolling back into a ball to stop any of the filling leaking. Use your palm to flatten slightly, then chill for 30 mins. Heat the oven to 200C/180C fan/gas 6.

4 Bake for 20 mins until golden. Cool on the tray for 15 mins. Move to a rack to cool completely.

5 Mix the icing sugar with the juice to a drizzling consistency. Drizzle over the biscuits, sprinkle with walnuts and zest, then allow to set. Will keep chilled in an airtight tin for up to 2 days.

Nutrition per serving
energy 336 kcals, fat 16g, saturates 9g, carbs 43g, sugars 24g, fibre 2g, protein 4g, salt 0.4g

Double-dipped peanut biscuits

Chocolate and peanut butter is a classic combination, and these double-dipped peanut biscuits really make the most of it.

 PREP 20 mins COOK 35 mins   MAKES 24

- 110g golden caster sugar
- 250g crunchy peanut butter
- 1 egg
- 100g white chocolate, chopped
- 100g dark chocolate, chopped

1 Heat the oven to 170C/150C fan/gas 3. Mix the sugar with the peanut butter and egg until it is thoroughly combined. Divide the mixture into 24 even balls. Line a couple of baking sheets with non-stick baking paper and put the balls on about 5cm apart. Press them down gently to uniform thickness. Bake for 35 minutes, or until lightly golden, don't over bake them or they'll get too hard. Cool completely.

2 Melt the chocolate in two separate bowls, either set over a pan of simmering water or in a microwave. Dip one half of each biscuit in the dark chocolate and let them set completely. Dip again into the white chocolate, leaving a border of dark chocolate. Leave to set.

Nutrition per serving
energy 133 kcals, fat 9g, saturates 3g, carbs 10g, sugars 9g, fibre 1g, protein 4g, salt 0.12g

Double-dipped shortbread biscuits

What could be better than shortbread biscuits? Shortbread double-dipped in milk and white chocolate! They're sure to go down a storm with family and friends.

 PREP 20 mins COOK 30 mins   MAKES 15

- 200g salted butter, softened
- 100g icing sugar
- 1 tsp vanilla extract
- 250g plain flour
- 1 tbsp milk, plus extra if needed
- 50g white chocolate, chopped
- 50g milk chocolate, chopped

YOU WILL NEED

- piping bag with a large star nozzle

1 Heat the oven to 180C/160C fan/gas 4. Beat the butter and icing sugar with an electric whisk until the mixture is light and fluffy. Beat in the vanilla and flour (the mixture will stiffen and look like crumble). Add the milk and keep beating until the mixture softens and sticks together (add more milk if needed).

2 Put into the piping bag and pipe swirled ring onto a baking sheet lined with parchment. If the mixture is stiff, roll the dough into balls an put on the sheet instead. The cookies spread so don't worry if there's a gap in the centre o the piped swirls but ensure there is enough space between each. Bake for 15 mins, or until lightly golden, then cool on a rack.

3 Heat the white and milk chocolate separate in the microwave or in bowls set over pans of simmering water. Dip the cookies into each chocolate, milk at one end and white on the other, then let excess drip off before returnin them to the rack to set. Will keep in an airtigh tin for up to 4 days.

Nutrition per serving
energy 224 kcals, fat 13g, saturates 8g, carbs 23g, sugars 10g, fibre 1g, protein 2g, salt 0.2g

Chapter 6

SAVOURY BISCUITS

· ·

Biscuits don't just come in the sweet variety; they can be made savoury too. Whether they're loaded with cheese or packed with chorizo (or both), these delectable bakes are perfect for everything from cheeseboards to midday snacks.

Manchego & chorizo melting biscuits

Bake a batch of these moreish smoky manchego and chorizo biscuits to serve as part of a cheeseboard.

 PREP 25 mins + chilling COOK 20 mins  MAKES 30

- 125g plain flour
- ½ tsp sweet smoked paprika
- 1 tsp fennel seeds, crushed
- 100g cold salted butter, cubed
- 100g manchego, grated
- 80g chorizo, very finely chopped

1 Put the flour, paprika and fennel seeds in a food processor and blitz with the butter until it resembles fine breadcrumbs. Add the manchego and chopped chorizo and blitz again until a dough forms. Roll into a 4cm log and wrap in parchment. Chill in the freezer for 30–40 mins until firm.

2 Heat the oven to 180C/160C fan/gas 4. Unwrap the dough and slice into 5mm-thick biscuits. Lay on a lined baking sheet well spaced apart (they will spread in the oven). Bake for 15–20 mins until golden. Leave to cool. Will keep in an airtight container for 3 days.

Nutrition per serving
energy 65 kcals, fat 5g, saturates 3g, carbs 3g, sugars 0.1g, fibre 0.2g, protein 2g, salt 0.2g

Cheese & rosemary biscuits

These savoury biscuits are deliciously cheesy and are so easy to make. They make a lovely gift. Leave out the rosemary if you prefer.

 PREP 25 mins COOK 14 mins MAKES 25

- 80g wholemeal flour
- 80g plain flour
- 100g cold butter, chopped
- 100g cheddar, finely grated
- 1 small rosemary sprig, leaves finely chopped
- 1 large egg yolk

YOU WILL NEED

- your choice of cookie cutters (optional)

1 Heat the oven to 180C/160C fan/gas 4. Put the flours in a bowl and rub in the butter until it resembles breadcrumbs. Stir in the cheese and rosemary, then add the yolk and mix in using a fork. When the mix starts to clump together, use your hands to knead to a smooth dough.

2 Roll out the dough between sheets of parchment and cut into shapes, then place on one or two lined baking trays and bake for 12–14 mins. Alternatively, take walnut-sized pieces of dough, roll into balls and place on the trays. Flatten slightly with a fork and bake as before. Cool on the baking trays for a few mins before moving to a rack to cool completely. Store in an airtight container for up to a week.

Nutrition per serving
energy 75 kcals, fat 5g, saturates 3g, carbs 5g, sugars 0.1g, fibre 1g, protein 2g, salt 0.2g

Sea salt water biscuits

Sensational spread with creamy cheese. Complete your cheeseboard with these homemade crackers.

 PREP 15 mins COOK 15 mins   MAKES 18

- 200g plain flour
- ½ tsp baking powder
- 50g cold butter, cut into cubes
- flaky sea salt

1 Heat the oven to 180C/160C fan/gas 4. Line two baking sheets with parchment. Place the flour, baking powder, butter and ½ tsp of the flaky salt in a food processor, then whizz for a minute until the butter is completely mixed with the flour. Add 4 tbsp water and pulse until the dough comes together. If it still feels dry, add 1 tsp more water and process until you have a soft but not sticky dough.

2 Roll out the dough on a lightly floured surface into a rectangle about 50 x 25cm and as thin as possible. Brush a little water over the surface of the dough, scatter 1 tsp salt flakes over and press in lightly. Prick the dough all over with a fork, then cut into 18 squares. Place on the prepared trays – don't worry if they stretch a bit. Bake for 10–15 mins until the biscuits feel dry and sandy but are still pale. They may still feel soft but will harden up when cooling. Transfer to a rack and leave until completely cool. Will keep in an airtight container for up to 2 weeks.

Nutrition per serving
energy 59 kcals, fat 2g, saturates 0g, carbs 9g, sugars 0g, fibre 0g, protein 1g, salt 0.36g

Cheese wheatmeal biscuits

Savoury oaty biscuits that are great for lunch boxes. Add yeast extract or peanut butter for a delicious pinwheel.

PREP 20 mins COOK 14 mins   MAKES 20–30

- 100g wholemeal flour
- 50g self-raising flour
- 25g medium oatmeal
- 100g butter
- 100g cheddar cheese, finely grated
- 1 large egg yolk

YOU WILL NEED
- your choice of cookie cutters (optional)

1 Heat the oven to 180C/160C fan/gas 4. Put the flours and oatmeal into a bowl and rub in the butter. Stir in the cheese. Add the egg yolk and mix in using a fork. When the mixture starts to clump together, use your hands to knead to a smooth dough.

2 Place the dough between two sheets of parchment and roll out thinly to about ½ cm. Cut out your desired shapes and lift them using a palette knife onto a non-stick baking sheet. Reroll any trimmings and cut out more shapes. Bake in the oven for 12–14 mins until golden brown. Leave on the tray for a few minutes to firm up before removing to a rack

3 Alternatively, take walnut-sized pieces of dough, roll into balls and place on the baking tray. Flatten slightly with a fork and bake as before.

Nutrition per serving
energy 90 kcals, fat 6.4g, saturates 3.8g, carbs 5.6g, sugars 0.2g, fibre 0.8g, protein 2.5g, salt 0.2g

Savoury biscotti

Serve these savoury biscotti on a cheeseboard and dunk them in a baked camembert or potted cheddar. They make a lovely gift too!

 PREP 25 mins COOK 1 hr 10 mins MAKES 40–45

- 350g plain flour, plus extra for dusting
- 2 tsp baking powder
- 60g golden caster sugar
- 3 large eggs, beaten
- 75g pitted black olives, chopped and patted dry with kitchen paper
- 8 thyme sprigs, leaves picked and chopped
- 40g parmesan

1 Heat the oven to 180C/160C fan/gas 4. Line two baking sheets with parchment. Mix the flour, baking powder, sugar, 1 tsp salt and a grinding of black pepper in a bowl. Stir in the eggs until the mix forms clumps, then bring together with hands into a dough. It will seem dry at first but keep kneading until no floury patches remain. Add the olives, thyme and parmesan, kneading until well distributed.

2 Tip the dough out onto a lightly floured surface and divide into four. With lightly floured hands, roll each into a sausage about 30cm long. Place two on each tray, well-spaced apart. Bake for 25–30 mins until risen and spread (it should still be pale). Remove, then cool on a rack for a few mins and turn down the oven to 140C/120C fan/gas 1.

3 Cut into 1cm thick slices on a sharp diagonal, then lay flat on the sheets. Bake for 20 mins, turn over, then bake for another 20 mins until dry and lightly golden. Transfer to a rack to cool. Will keep in an airtight tin for 1 month.

Nutrition per serving
energy 45 kcals, fat 1g, saturates 0.3g, carbs 7g, sugars 1g, fibre 0.4g, protein 2g, salt 0.3g

Seeded oatcakes

These quick biscuits make a great addition to a cheeseboard or gourmet homemade gift hamper.

 PREP 15 mins COOK 15 mins   MAKES 20

- 50g butter
- 100g medium oatmeal
- 100g plain flour, plus extra for dusting
- 1 tsp bicarbonate of soda
- 2 tsp poppy seeds
- 2 tbsp sesame seeds

1 Heat the oven to 200C/180C fan/gas 6. Melt the butter in a small pan, then allow to cool slightly. Tip all the dry ingredients into a bowl, with ½ tsp salt, then pour in the butter. Add 5–6 tbsp boiling water and combine to make a firm dough.

2 Turn out the dough onto a lightly floured surface, then roll out until about ½ cm thick. Cut into small squares and bake for 12–15 mins until golden. Leave to cool for a few mins, then transfer to a rack and cool completely.

Nutrition per serving
energy 63 kcals, fat 3.5g, saturates 1.5g, carbs 7g, sugars 0.1g, fibre 0.6g, protein 1.4g, salt 0.3g

Cheddar & hazelnut shortbread

Hazelnuts and cheese are perfect together – rustle up these savoury shortbread biscuits with just five ingredients. They make a great mid-afternoon snack.

 PREP 15 mins + chilling COOK 20 mins   MAKES 40

- 155g blanched hazelnuts
- 110g cold butter, cut into chunks
- 100g plain flour
- 225g mature cheddar, finely grated
- 1 medium egg, lightly beaten

1 Blitz 85g of the hazelnuts in a food processor until ground. Cut the rest of the hazelnuts in half.

2 Pulse the ground hazelnuts, butter, flour, cheddar, ½ tsp salt and the egg in the food processor a few times. Don't pulse for too long – you want the mixture to look like breadcrumbs rather than coming together in a ball. Tip the mixture onto a large piece of cling film and, using the cling film to shape it, mould it into a ball, then leave in the fridge for a couple of hours.

3 Heat the oven to 200C/180C fan/gas 6. Pull off chunks of the dough – about a tablespoon at a time – and roll each piece into a ball. Place on a baking sheet and flatten to 3.5cm across, leaving room between each one. Push 3–4 hazelnut halves into each biscuit. Cook for 10 mins, or until the biscuits are golden brown. Leave to cool on the baking sheet, then transfer to a rack. Will keep for up to 3 days in an airtight container.

Nutrition per serving
energy 81 kcals, fat 7g, saturates 3g, carbs 2g, sugars 0g, fibre 0g, protein 2g, salt 0.2g

Homemade rosemary crackers

These rosemary crackers are addictive! The dough is just a simple mix of flour, water and oil, into which you can add a flavour, such as rosemary or thyme.

 PREP 10 mins COOK 15 mins SERVES 6

- 150g plain flour
- 1 tsp flaky sea salt
- 1 tsp golden caster sugar
- 1 tbsp finely chopped rosemary, plus 1 tsp for sprinkling on top
- 80ml water mixed with 2 tbsp olive oil

1 Heat your oven to 220C/200C fan/gas 7. Put all the ingredients in a bowl and mix with your hands to combine to a rough dough. If it's sticky, add a little more flour so it's nice and smooth.

2 On a sheet of parchment sprinkled with flour, roll the dough out to the thickness of a £1 coin, then use a pizza cutter or knife and cut it into squares.

3 Brush the squares with a little water and sprinkle with some salt and the 1 tsp chopped rosemary. Prick each square once in the middle with a fork.

4 Transfer the parchment straight onto a baking sheet, separate each square of dough a little and bake in the hot oven for 12–15 mins or until the crackers are slightly golden. Cool, then store in a tin for up to 2 weeks.

Nutrition per serving
energy 129 kcals, fat 4g, saturates 1g, carbs 20g, sugars 1g, fibre 1g, protein 2g, salt 1.2g

Chapter 7

BISCUIT BARS & DESSERTS

· ·

There's an endless possibility of desserts you can use biscuits in and we wanted to share with you some of our favourites. These are particularly great for using up any leftover biscuits you may have to save them going to waste.

Giant cookie

. . . .

You'll love this giant cookie that's very versatile. You can adapt with your favourite treats like marshmallows, pretzels, nuts, toffee or fudge.

🕐 PREP 15 mins COOK 20 mins 📑 SERVES 6–8

- 200g butter at room temperature, plus extra for the pan
- 250g light brown sugar
- 2 egg yolks
- ½ tsp vanilla extract
- 275g plain flour
- 1 tsp baking powder
- 150g chocolate chips
- 100g other cookie fillings, such as pretzels, chopped nuts, pieces of fudge or toffee, marshmallows
- vanilla ice cream, to serve (optional)

1 Heat the oven to 180C/160C fan/gas 4. Tip the butter and sugar into a large mixing bowl, beat until combined, then stir in the yolks and vanilla. Tip in the flour, baking powder, chocolate chips, a pinch of sea salt and any other fillings you want to add. Mix until a crumbly dough forms.

2 Lightly butter a 25cm ovenproof frying pan. Spoon in and flatten the cookie mixture. For a gooey dessert, bake for 20 mins, leave to rest for 5 mins, then scoop straight from the pan and serve with ice cream, if you like. For a firmer cookie you can cut, bake for 30 mins, then leave to cool completely before cutting into wedges.

. . . .

Nutrition per serving
energy 596 kcals, fat 29g, saturates 17g, carbs 76g, sugars 40g, fibre 2g, protein 7g, salt 0.2g

Nanaimo bars

These bars from Canada are so moreish, with a crunchy biscuit base, custard layer and chocolate topping.

 PREP 25 mins + chilling + setting COOK 5 mins   SERVES 16

FOR THE BISCUIT BASE
- 125g softened butter
- 50g caster sugar
- 5 tbsp cocoa powder
- 1 egg, beaten
- 200g digestive biscuits, blitzed to crumbs
- 100g desiccated coconut
- 50g chopped almonds (optional)

FOR THE CUSTARD ICING
- 100g butter, softened
- 4 tbsp double cream
- 3 tbsp custard powder
- 250g icing sugar

FOR THE CHOCOLATE TOPPING
- 150g dark chocolate
- 50g butter

1 Start by making the biscuit base. In a bowl, over a pan of simmering water, melt the butter with the sugar and cocoa powder, stirring occasionally until smooth. Whisk in the egg for 2–3 mins until the mixture has thickened. Remove from heat and mix in the biscuit crumbs, coconut and almonds, if using, then press into the base of a lined 20cm square tin. Chill for 10 mins.

2 For the middle layer, make the custard icing. Whisk the butter, cream and custard powder until light and fluffy, then gradually add the icing sugar until incorporated. Spread over the bottom layer and chill in the fridge for at least 10 mins until the custard is no longer soft.

3 Melt the chocolate and butter together in the microwave or in a bowl over a pan of simmering water, then spread over the chilled bars and put back in the fridge. Leave until the chocolate has fully set (about 2 hrs). Take the mixture out of the tin and slice into squares to serve.

Nutrition per serving
energy 415 kcals, fat 29g, saturates 18g, carbs 33g, sugars 23g, fibre 0g, protein 3g, salt 0.6g

PBJ cookie ice cream sandwiches

Kids – and adults! – will love these ice cream sandwiches. Raspberry ice cream is sandwiched between two peanut butter cookies for the ultimate decadent dessert

 PREP 20 mins + overnight freezing   COOK 12 mins   MAKES 8 plus 500ml ice cream

FOR THE ICE CREAM
- 120g frozen raspberries
- 1 lemon, juiced
- 2 tbsp icing sugar
- ½ tbsp liquid glucose (optional)
- ½ x 397g can condensed milk
- 600ml double cream
- 1 tsp vanilla bean paste

FOR THE COOKIES
- 200g peanut butter
- 50g golden caster sugar
- 125g light brown soft sugar
- 1 egg

1 Tip the berries into a food processor with the juice, sugar and glucose, if using. Blitz until smooth. Push the raspberries through a fine mesh sieve into a bowl. Whisk the rest of the ingredients in another bowl for 5 mins until thick, then add to a freezerproof container or large loaf tin. Ripple through the purée using a skewer. Cover and freeze overnight.

2 Heat the oven to 180C/160C fan/gas 4. Line two large baking sheets with parchment. Mix the peanut butter and sugars in a bowl with a large pinch of salt. Beat in the egg until you have a stiff dough. Break off cherry-tomato-sized lumps of dough (you should get about 16) and arrange on the sheets, well-spaced apart. Press the cookies down with the back of a fork. Bake for 10–12 mins until golden. Leave to cool on the sheets. Once cool, sandwich a scoop of ice cream between two cookies just before serving (you should use half the ice cream). The remaining 500ml ice cream will keep frozen for 3 months.

Nutrition per serving
energy 490 kcals, fat 35g, saturates 17g, carbs 34g, sugars 32g, fibre 2g, protein 9g, salt 0.3g

Citrus bars

A crisp shortbread biscuit base with a creamy citrus curd baked onto the top.

 PREP 20 mins COOK:45 mins   MAKES 18

FOR THE BASE
- 250g plain flour
- 85g icing sugar, plus extra for dusting
- 175g butter, cut into small pieces

FOR THE TOPPING
- 4 large eggs
- 400g caster sugar
- 2 lemons and 1 large orange, zested and juiced
- 50g plain flour

1 Heat the oven to 180C/160C fan/gas 4. Line the base and sides of a shallow rectangular tin (about 23 x 33cm) with parchment. Whizz the flour, sugar and butter to fine crumbs in a food processor. Tip into the prepared tin and smoothly level, pressing it down lightly. Bake for 20–25 mins until pale golden.

2 To make the topping, whisk the eggs and sugar using an electric whisk for 1 min, then add the citrus zest and 120ml juice and whisk again briefly. Sift in the flour and whisk well to mix. Pour over the shortbread and bake for 15–20 mins until the topping has just set. Cool completely in the tin, then lift out of the tin using the lining paper. Dust thickly with icing sugar and cut into 3 down the length and 6 across to make 18 bars.

Nutrition per serving
energy 257 kcals, fat 10g, saturates 6g, carbs 39g, sugars 28g, fibre 1g, protein 3g, salt 0.2g

Cookie base classic s'mores

Ever tried an American-style marshmallow s'more? It's a Bonfire Night-friendly stack of sweet joy, with cookies and chocolate spread thrown in for good measure.

 PREP 5 mins COOK 1 min MAKES 8

- 16 chocolate chip cookies
- 8 marshmallows (vegetarian brand, if required)
- 8 tsp chocolate hazelnut spread

1 Preheat the grill to high and line a baking sheet with parchment. Put eight cookies on the tray and top each with a marshmallow. Grill until the marshmallow begins to brown and melt.
2 Put a tsp of chocolate hazelnut spread on the other eight cookies and sandwich on top of the melty marshmallow layer.

Nutrition per serving
energy 194 kcals, fat 8g, saturates 4g, carbs 27g, sugars 16g, fibre 0.2g, protein 2g, salt 0.3g

Fifteens

· ·

Good Food reader Alice Colley shares her recipe for this Northern Irish fridge cake with digestives, marshmallows and glacé cherries.

 PREP 20 mins + chilling    MAKES 15

- 15 digestive biscuits
- 15 marshmallows
- 15 glacé cherries, cut in half
- about 200ml condensed milk
- 100g desiccated coconut, to coat

1 Crush the digestive biscuits in a food processor or in a plastic bag with a rolling pin, then put them in a large mixing bowl. Chop each marshmallow into four pieces and add to the bowl with the cherries and 175ml of the condensed milk. Mix until the ingredients are well combined and you have a sticky mixture. If it's too dry, add a splash more condensed milk.

2 Sprinkle most of the coconut over a large piece of cling film (or foil). Tip the mixture onto the coconut and shape into a long sausage, about 30 x 5cm. Sprinkle more coconut over the top of it and wrap the cling film tightly around, twisting the ends together. Leave in the fridge to chill for 4–6 hrs, then cut into 15 slices and serve. Will keep in the fridge for up to 1 week wrapped in cling film.

· ·

Nutrition per serving
energy 229 kcals, fat 12g, saturates 9g, carbs 25g, sugars 17g, fibre 2g, protein 3g, salt 0.3g

Easy rocky road

• •

Great for a bake sale, a gift or simply an afternoon treat to enjoy with a cuppa, this rocky road is quick to make and uses mainly store cupboard ingredients.

 PREP 15 mins + chilling COOK 5 mins   MAKES 12

- 200g digestive biscuits (rich tea can also be used)
- 135g butter or margarine
- 200g dark chocolate (70% cocoa works best)
- 2–3 tbsp golden syrup
- 100g mini marshmallows (chopped regular marshmallows work too)
- icing sugar, to dust

OPTIONAL (UP TO 100G)
- raisins, dried cranberries or any dried fruit
- nuts
- popcorn
- honeycomb, broken into pieces

1 Grease and line an 18cm square brownie tin with baking paper.
2 Place the digestive biscuits in a freezer bag and bash with a rolling pin or just the side of your fist until they're broken into a mixture of everything between dust and 50p-sized lumps. Set aside.
3 In a large saucepan, melt the butter or margarine, dark chocolate and golden syrup over a gentle heat, stirring constantly until there are no or almost no more lumps of chocolate visible, then remove from the heat. Leave to cool.
4 Take the biscuits, mini marshmallows and up to 100g of additional ingredients (dried fruit, nuts, popcorn, honeycomb), if you like, and stir into the chocolate mixture until everything is completely covered.
5 Tip the mixture into the lined baking tin and spread it out to the corners. Chill for at least 2 hrs then dust with icing sugar and cut into 12 fingers.

• •

Nutrition per serving
energy 320 kcals, fat 20g, saturates 11g, carbs 31g, sugars 20g, fibre 3g, protein 3g, salt 0.5g

Chapter 8

AFTERNOON TEA BISCUITS

· ·

Hosting your own afternoon tea is a wonderful way to bring friends and family together. Why not add some biscuits to your tea that are simple to make and can be done in advance? These delicate, dainty sweet snacks will be the perfect accompaniment to any afternoon tea you host.

Florentine biscuits

We've given the classic Florentine a chocolate-covered biscuity base, so they're perfect for dunking at an afternoon tea.

 PREP 55 mins + chilling COOK 25 mins   MAKES 36

FOR THE BISCUIT BASE
- 175g slightly salted butter, softened
- 85g golden caster sugar
- ½ tsp vanilla extract
- 225g plain flour, plus extra for dusting
- ¼ tsp ground cinnamon

FOR THE FLORENTINE TOPPING
- 50g butter
- 50g light brown soft sugar
- 50g golden syrup
- ½ tsp salt
- 50g plain flour
- 75g glacé cherries, chopped
- 75g flaked almonds
- 150g dark chocolate, chopped

YOU WILL NEED
- 1 x 6cm fluted cookie cutter

1 To make the biscuits, beat the butter, sugar and vanilla with an electric whisk until creamy. Add the flour and cinnamon and combine with a spatula. Form into a ball, wrap in cling film and chill for at least 1 hr.

2 Melt the butter, sugar, syrup and salt. Remove from the heat and whisk in the flour, then stir in the cherries and almonds. Leave to cool and firm up. Heat the oven to 180C/160C fan, gas 4 and line a baking sheet with parchment.

3 Tip the dough onto a floured work surface and roll out to the thickness of a £1 coin. Stamp out circles, then re-roll the trimmings and stamp more. Transfer to the baking sheet and spoon on the Florentine mixture. Bake for 12–15 mins until golden and the topping has melted. Cool on the sheet for at least 15 mins.

4 Melt the chocolate in a small heatproof bowl over a pan of simmering water or in the microwave. Dip each biscuit about a third of the way in, then return to the sheet to set. Will keep for up to 4 days in a sealed container.

Nutrition per serving
energy 137 kcals, fat 8g, saturates 4g, carbs 14g, sugars 6g, fibre 1g, protein 2g, salt 0.2g

Easy biscotti

Make these easy biscotti to serve with coffee or dip into chocolate for a twist on a classic recipe.

 PREP 20 mins + cooling COOK 50 mins   MAKES 20

- 300g plain flour
- 100g caster sugar
- 50g light brown soft sugar
- 1½ tsp baking powder
- 80ml vegetable oil
- 1 large egg
- 2 tsp vanilla extract
- milk or dark chocolate, melted, to decorate (optional)

1 Heat the oven to 180C/160C fan/gas 4 and line a baking tray with parchment. Put the flour, sugars, baking powder and a large pinch of salt in a large bowl and stir together

2 In a separate bowl, whisk together the oil, egg, vanilla and 3 tbsp hot water. Gradually mix the wet ingredients into the dry until a dough forms, then gently knead until smooth It will be quite dry, so add another 1 tbsp water if it's too difficult to knead after a few minutes. Shape the dough into two 25 x 8cm logs. Put on the baking tray and bake for 25–30 mins. Cool on the tray for 15 mins.

3 Cut the cooled logs into 1–2cm-thick slices crossways. Return the biscotti to the lined baking tray and bake for 15–20 mins more, turning the tray halfway through. Cool slight on the tray, then transfer to a rack to cool completely. If you like, dip one end of each into melted chocolate, then leave to set on baking tray lined with parchment. Will keep an airtight container for up to 5 days.

Nutrition per serving
energy 127 kcals, fat 5g, saturates 0g, carbs 19g, sugars 8g, fibre 1g, protein 2g, salt 0.15g

Cardamom & pistachio biscuits

Everyone will love these beautiful biscuits and they make an impressive part of an afternoon tea. Dip them in chocolate and sprinkles to finish.

 PREP 15 mins + chilling + setting COOK 25 mins   MAKES 40

- 200g unsalted butter, at room temperature
- 400g plain flour, plus extra for dusting
- 150g golden caster sugar
- 50g runny honey
- ¼ tsp rosewater
- 1 egg
- a pinch of salt
- 5 cardamom pods, shelled and crushed
- ½ teaspoon cream of tartar

TO DECORATE
- 100g dark chocolate
- choice of sprinkles – we used dried rose petals, chopped pistachios, desiccated coconut and orange zest

1 Rub the butter and the flour together with your fingertips until it looks like grainy sand.

2 In another bowl, stir the rest of the ingredient until smooth and runny. Pour over the butter/ flour mix and combine with your hands. Whe the dough is soft and squidgy, shape into a ball, wrap in cling film and chill for 20–30 min

3 Before you remove the dough from the fridge heat your oven to 180C/160C fan/gas 4 and line two baking sheets with parchment.

4 Sprinkle flour on your work surface and rolling pin and roll out the dough until it's as thick as a £1 coin. Use your ruler and a dinner knife to cut 10 x 3cm rectangles and put on the trays leaving space between each biscuit.

5 Bake for 10–12 mins, then cool on the trays for a few minutes. Transfer to a rack.

6 Melt the chocolate in a heatproof bowl over a pan of simmering water or in a microwave then dip the end of each biscuit and leave t set on a plate. Before they set, sprinkle with your toppings and leave for 1–2 hrs to set. These biscuits keep for 2–3 days.

Nutrition per serving
energy 94 kcals, fat 4g, saturates 3g, carbs 12g, sugars 5g, fibre 0g, protein 1g, salt 0.g

Baci di dama

Nicknamed 'lady's kisses', these little Italian biscuits made with hazelnuts and chocolate are the perfect accompaniment to an afternoon tea.

 PREP 15 mins + chilling + setting COOK 20 mins  MAKES 16 biscuits

- 100g blanched hazelnuts, toasted
- 100g butter
- 100g caster sugar
- 100g flour (preferably '00' flour)

FOR THE FILLING
- 100g dark chocolate, broken into small pieces

1 Blitz the hazelnuts to fine crumbs, but be careful not to over-blitz – you don't want them to become oily. Add the butter and sugar, and blitz again until really creamy, then tip the mixture into a bowl and sift in the flour. Mix with your hands, then chill in the fridge for an hour or until firm enough to roll.

2 Heat the oven to 180C/160C fan/gas 4 and line a large baking sheet with parchment. Tear off teaspoon-sized chunks of mixture and roll into balls, then place on the sheet around 2cm apart. Bake for 15 mins until golden brown, then transfer to a rack to cool.

3 To make the filling, heat the chocolate in a bowl in the microwave, stirring every 10 secs until fully melted. Spread a small spoonful of chocolate on half the cooled biscuits. Leave to set for about 15 mins then sandwich the remaining biscuits on top. Leave the baci di dama to set completely (put them in the fridge if the kitchen is warm). Serve the biscuits with coffee.

Nutrition per serving
energy 173 kcals, fat 12g, saturates 5g, carbs 14g, sugars 8g, fibre 1g, protein 2g, salt 0.12g

Hazelnut crisps

These thin and delicate nutty biscuits are delicious served with ice cream or creamy desserts or presented in a gift hamper.

 PREP 25 mins COOK 10 mins  MAKES about 30

- 85g hazelnuts
- 50g plain flour
- 200g caster sugar
- 2 egg whites
- ½ tsp vanilla extract

1 Heat the oven to 200C/180C fan/gas 6. Line two large baking sheets with parchment. Toast the hazelnuts in a dry frying pan, then grind in a food processor or mini chopper until roughly ground. Mix the flour, sugar and ground nuts. Whisk the egg whites to soft peaks, then fold into the dry ingredients with the vanilla.

2 Drop tsps of the mixture, spaced apart, onto the lined baking sheets. Bake for 8–10 mins until just starting to colour. Let cool for 10 mins, then remove and cool completely o a rack. Store in a tin for up to 3 weeks.

Nutrition per serving
energy 51 kcals, fat 2g, saturates 0g, carbs 8g, sugars 7g, fibre 0g, protein 1g, salt 0g

Alfajores

These melt-in-the-mouth shortbread-like cookies originate from South America and are filled with dulce de leche and rolled in desiccated coconut.

 PREP 45 mins + chilling COOK 8 mins   MAKES 30

- 200g plain flour
- 300g cornflour
- 2 tsp baking powder
- 250g unsalted butter, softened at room temperature
- 150g caster sugar
- zest of 1 lemon
- 3 large egg yolks
- 1 tbsp cognac
- 1 tsp vanilla extract
- 450g jar dulce de leche
- 50g desiccated coconut

YOU WILL NEED
- 1 x 5cm round or fluted cookie cutter

1 Combine the flour, cornflour and baking powder together in a bowl with a pinch of salt. Using a food mixer or an electric whisk in another bowl, beat the butter together with the sugar and lemon zest until very pale. Add the egg yolks followed by the cognac and vanilla extract. Beat in the dry ingredients until you have smooth dough. Wrap the dough in cling film and chill for a minimum of 1 hour. You can make the biscuit dough the day before and leave in the fridge.

2 Line two large baking trays with parchment. Roll out the dough on a lightly floured surface to the thickness of a £1 coin then cut out 60 biscuits. Put the biscuits in the fridge for 20 mins to firm up.

3 Heat the oven to 180C/160C fan/gas 4. Bake for 8 mins until just set. You want the biscuits t stay pale with a crumbly texture. Cool completely before sandwiching the biscuits together with a spoonful of dulce de leche. Once they are all sandwiched, roll in cocont

Nutrition per serving
energy 157 kcals, fat 7g, saturates 5g, carbs 21g, sugars 9g, fibre 0.4g, protein 2g, salt 0.1g

Coconut biscuits

• •

Make these coconut biscuits for the perfect pick-me-up. They're coated in luxurious dark chocolate and toasted coconut sprinkles.

 PREP 20 mins + setting COOK 15 mins   MAKES 14–16

- 200g unsalted butter, softened
- 75g caster sugar
- 75g light brown soft sugar
- 1 tsp vanilla bean paste
- 1 large egg
- 275g plain flour
- 125g desiccated coconut, toasted and cooled
- 100g dark chocolate

1 Heat the oven to 190C/170C fan/gas 5. Beat the butter in a large bowl using an electric whisk or in a stand mixer until very soft. Beat in both sugars and the vanilla until light and fluffy, then beat in the egg until just combined. Sift in the flour and a pinch of salt and stir to combine. Fold in 100g of the toasted coconut.

2 Roll the dough into 14–16 balls (about 45g each) and arrange on a baking sheet lined with parchment, spaced apart. Flatten each slightly using the palm of your hand and bake for 12–15 mins until golden and slightly firm to the touch. Leave to cool on the sheet briefly, then transfer to a rack to cool completely.

3 Melt the chocolate in the microwave or in a bowl set over a pan of simmering water. Dip one half of each biscuit into the melted chocolate, then lay on a sheet of parchment and sprinkle with the remaining toasted coconut. Leave to set for about 30 mins.

• •

Nutrition per serving
energy 285 kcals, fat 18g, saturates 12g, carbs 26g, sugars 12g, fibre 3g, protein 3g, salt 0.03g

Almond biscuits

These amaretti-style biscuits use minimal flour and have a light, airy finish, perfect to accompany tea or eat with a fruit mousse or fool.

 PREP 15 mins COOK 20 mins   MAKES 34

- 4 egg whites
- 140g caster sugar
- 2 tbsp plain flour
- 140g ground almonds

1 Heat the oven to 160C/140C fan/gas 3. Line two baking trays with parchment. Place the egg whites in a clean bowl and whisk until they form soft peaks. Add the sugar and continue to whisk for a few mins more until the whites are glossy. Sift the flour onto the whites spoon over the almonds, then fold everything together quickly, keeping the mixture light and airy.

2 Spoon tbsp of the almond mix, well spaced apart, onto the prepared trays. Bake for 20 mins until golden. Remove from the oven and cool on a rack. These biscuits are best freshly baked but will keep in a sealed container for up to a week.

Nutrition per serving
energy 47 kcals, fat 2g, saturates 0g, carbs 5g, sugars 4g, fibre 0g, protein 1g, salt 0g

Viennese whirls

• •

These elegant, buttery biscuits might look impressive but they're surprisingly easy to make. Dip in chocolate for an extra sweet treat.

 PREP 45 mins COOK 12 mins   MAKES 10

FOR THE BISCUITS
- 200g slightly salted butter, softened
- 50g icing sugar
- 2 tsp vanilla extract
- 200g plain flour
- 2 tsp cornflour
- ½ tsp baking powder

FOR THE FILLING
- 100g butter, softened
- 170g icing sugar
- 1 tsp vanilla extract
- 50g raspberry jam or strawberry jam

YOU WILL NEED
- 2 x piping bags, one with a large star nozzle

1 Heat the oven to 180C/160C fan/gas 4 and line two baking sheets with parchment. Beat the butter and icing sugar with an electric hand whisk for about 5 mins until pale and fluffy. Add the vanilla and beat again.

2 Sift in the flour, cornflour and baking powder and fold in with a spatula. Spoon into the piping bag (you may have to pipe in batches

3 Pipe swirly 5cm circles on the baking sheets, leaving 3cm spaces between each swirl.

4 Bake for 10–12 mins, swapping the trays over halfway, until pale golden. Cool on the sheet for a few mins, then transfer to racks.

5 Stir the butter and icing sugar together, initially with a wooden spoon, then switch to electric beaters or a whisk to get the buttercream fluffy and smooth. Add the vanilla and beat once more. Transfer to the other piping bag and snip off the end.

6 Turn the biscuits over so their flat side is facing up, then pipe buttercream over half and spread jam on the rest. Sandwich together.

• •

Nutrition per serving
energy 405 kcals, fat 25g, saturates 16g, carbs 42g, sugars 25g, fibre 1g, protein 2g, salt 0.6g

Coconut macaroons

Make these light coconut macaroons with just a handful of ingredients. They look impressive but are deceptively simple, quick and easy to make.

 PREP 30 mins + setting COOK 15 mins   MAKES 10-12

- 2 eggs, whites only
- 80g caster sugar
- 150g desiccated coconut
- 1 tsp vanilla paste
- 90g dark chocolate

1 Whisk together the egg whites and caster sugar in a large bowl for 2–3 mins until light and frothy and the sugar has dissolved. Add the coconut, a pinch of salt and the vanilla, then stir until combined. Leave to stand for 10 mins.

2 Heat the oven to 170C/150C fan/gas 3. Line a baking sheet with parchment. Scoop teaspoonfuls of the mix into balls and arrange on the sheet. Bake for 10–12 mins until golden.

3 Leave on the sheet to cool completely. Melt the chocolate in a heatproof bowl over a pan of simmering water or in the microwave. Tip the melted chocolate into a bowl, then dip the bottom of each cooled macaroon into the chocolate and wipe off any excess. Arrange on a sheet of parchment, chocolate side up, then put in the fridge for 20 mins, or until set. You can use any remaining melted chocolate to pipe zigzags over the top, if you like, then leave to set.

Nutrition per serving
energy 154 kcals, fat 11g, saturates 8g, carbs 10g, sugars 9g, fibre 3g, protein 2g, salt 0.14g

Lemon biscuits

Who could resist a zesty treat? These dainty melt-in-the-mouth lemon biscuits make a scrumptious addition to an afternoon tea spread.

 PREP 30 mins COOK 12 mins   MAKES 20

- 200g soft butter
- 140g caster sugar
- 1 egg yolk
- 1 tsp vanilla extract
- zest 2 lemons, juice 1
- 280g plain flour, plus a little extra for rolling
- ½ jar good lemon curd
- 140g icing sugar, sifted

YOU WILL NEED
- 1 x 5–6cm round cookie cutter

1 Stir together the butter, sugar, egg yolk, vanilla and zest from 1 lemon using a wooden spoon. Stir in the flour – you might need to get your hands in at the end. Tip onto a floured surface, bring together into a smooth dough then roll out, half at a time, and stamp out rounds. Keep re-rolling trimmings, you should get about 40 biscuits. Arrange on trays lined with parchment, cover with cling film and chill for 30 mins.

2 Heat the oven to 200C/180C fan/gas 6. Bake the biscuits for 8–12 mins until pale golden, then cool. Once cool, spread half the biscuits with a little lemon curd and top with a second biscuit. Arrange the biscuits on racks over trays. Mix enough lemon juice into the icing sugar to give a runny consistency, then drizzle over the biscuits. Scatter over a bit more lemon zest and leave to set.

Nutrition per serving
energy 202 kcals, fat 8g, saturates 5g, carbs 31g, sugars 18g, fibre 1g, protein 1g, salt 0.14g

Caramelised honey and tahini cookies

Use up that jar of sesame paste in the back of your cupboard to bake these decadent honey and tahini biscuits. They're sweet, salty and totally addictive.

 PREP 20 mins + chilling COOK 10 mins   MAKES 18

- 150g honey
- 150g salted butter, cubed
- 75g dark brown soft sugar
- 75g caster sugar
- 100g tahini
- 1 large egg, plus 1 large yolk
- 250g plain flour
- ¼ tsp bicarbonate of soda
- 1 tsp sea salt flakes
- 1 tbsp mixed black & white sesame seeds

1 Bring the honey to a boil in a pan set over a medium-high heat. Boil for 5 mins until it has darkened and smells nutty – this adds flavour. Whisk briefly, then remove from the heat and whisk in the butter until melted. Transfer to a heatproof bowl and leave to cool.

2 Tip both the sugars, tahini, egg and yolk into the bowl with the honey mix, then beat to combine. In another bowl, mix the flour and bicarb, then pour the wet ingredients into the dry and mix until it comes together into a dough. Chill for 3 hrs, or overnight.

3 Heat the oven to 180C/160C fan/gas 4 and line two baking trays with parchment. Roll the dough into 18 balls (about 45g each) and arrange on the trays, spaced 5cm apart. Press down with the back of a spoon to slightly flatten the tops, then sprinkle over the sea salt and sesame seeds and bake for 10–12 mins.

4 Tap the tray on a work surface to slightly flatten the cookies. Leave to cool for 10 mins, then transfer to a rack to cool completely. Will keep in an airtight container for 3 days.

Nutrition per serving
energy 217 kcals. fat 11g. saturates 5g. carbs 25g. sugars 14g. fibre 1g. protein 3g. salt 0.5g

Chapter 9

VEGAN & GLUTEN-FREE BISCUITS

....

Here are some of our favourite gluten-free and vegan recipes, which are perfect for anyone with dietary requirements who doesn't want to compromise on flavour. These recipes are simple to make and perfect to have in the freezer in case any guests come around with special requirements.

Vegan chocolate chip cookies

Try our best-ever vegan chocolate chip cookies. Non-vegans will be hard pressed to notice the difference between these and their favourite choc chip biscuits.

 PREP 15 mins + chilling COOK 15 mins   MAKES 20

- 125g cold coconut oil
- 100g golden caster sugar
- 150g light muscovado sugar
- 125ml coconut milk
- 1 tsp vanilla extract
- 275g plain flour
- 1 tsp baking powder
- ¼ tsp bicarb
- 200g vegan chocolate chips or vegan chocolate, chopped into small chunks

1 Tip the coconut oil and sugars into a bowl and whisk until completely combined, then whisk in the coconut milk and vanilla. Tip the flour, baking powder, bicarb and a good pinch of flaky sea salt into the mix to make a thick batter, then fold through the chocolate chips. Chill the batter for at least 1 hr. Can be made 2 days ahead.

2 Heat the oven to 180C/160C fan/gas 4. Line a couple of baking sheets with parchment, then scoop or roll plum-sized balls of the dough and place them on the baking sheet, about 2cm apart. Flatten ever so slightly and sprinkle with a bit more flaky salt if you want. Cook on the middle shelf for 12–15 mins, turning the tray once, until the cookies have spread and are golden but still soft in the middle. Leave to cool slightly, then lift the cookies onto a rack while you bake another batch. Will keep in a biscuit jar for up to 3 days.

Nutrition per serving
energy 221 kcals, fat 10g, saturates 8g, carbs 29g, sugars 19g, fibre 1g, protein 2g, salt 0.12g

Vegan peanut butter cookies

Make some moreish vegan peanut butter cookies for a welcome mid-morning treat. Made with dairy-free ingredients, they're sure to be loved by all.

 PREP 20 mins + chilling COOK 15 mins MAKES 10

- 100g dairy-free margarine
- 100g caster sugar
- 2 tbsp vanilla paste
- 100g crunchy peanut butter
- 225g plain flour
- 3 tbsp roasted peanuts, split in half

YOU WILL NEED
- 1 x 8cm round cookie cutter

1 Beat the margarine, sugar and vanilla using an electric whisk for 1 min until pale and smooth, then mix in the peanut butter and flour until fully incorporated. Bring together into a smooth dough with your hands.

2 Roll out the dough between two sheets of parchment until it's about 1cm thick. If the dough is very soft (this will depend on the margarine used), chill for 45 mins until firmed slightly. Heat the oven to 160C/140C fan/gas and line one large or two medium baking trays with parchment.

3 Cut circles out of the dough, placing the rounds on the lined baking trays. Press a few peanut halves, cut side up, firmly into the top of the biscuits. Bake for 12–15 mins until turning lightly golden around the edges. Leave to cool on the trays for 5 mins, then lift onto a rack to cool completely.

Nutrition per serving
energy 270 kcals, fat 14g, saturates 3g, carbs 29g, sugars 11g, fibre 2g, protein 7g, salt 0.3g

Vegan shortbread

Make our vegan shortbread with olive oil for a buttery flavour and cornflour to get the crumbliness of traditional versions. They taste great with nut butter.

 PREP 20 mins + chilling COOK 20 mins   MAKES 12–14

- 250g plain flour, plus extra for dusting
- 75g caster sugar, plus 1 tbsp
- ½ tbsp cornflour
- 1 tsp vanilla extract
- 160ml light olive oil

YOU WILL NEED
- 1 x 6cm round or fluted cookie cutter

1 Whizz the flour, sugar, a pinch of salt and the cornflour in a food processor to sieve and mix briefly, then add the vanilla and drizzle in the olive oil, pulsing the food processor blades until you get a soft, golden dough. Wrap and chill for 30 mins to rest.

2 Heat the oven to 180C/160C fan/gas 4 and line a baking sheet with parchment or a baking mat. Roll the dough out on a lightly floured work surface to a 5mm thickness and cut out shortbread rounds. Use a small palette knife to transfer to the baking sheet. They can be frozen on the baking tray, then transferred to a box when solid. Will keep for up to 3 months.

3 Sprinkle the 1 tbsp sugar over the biscuits and bake for 15–20 mins until golden brown. Leave to cool for a few mins to firm up on the tray, then transfer to a rack to cool completely. Add 2–4 mins to the cooking time if baking from frozen.

Nutrition per serving
energy 176 kcals, fat 9g, saturates 1g, carbs 21g, sugars 7g, fibre 1g, protein 2g, salt 0.03g

Vegan gingerbread cookies

Switch the butter for coconut oil, eggs for chia and use chickpea water in royal icing to make these easy, totally vegan Christmas gingerbread biscuits.

 PREP 30 mins COOK 12 mins   MAKES around 20

- 1 tbsp chia seeds
- 400g plain flour, plus extra for dusting
- 200g coconut oil
- 2 tbsp ground ginger
- 1 tsp ground cinnamon
- 200g dark muscovado sugar
- 50g maple syrup
- 100ml aquafaba (water from a can of chickpeas)
- 500g icing sugar
- ½ tsp lemon juice

YOU WILL NEED

- 1 x gingerbread person cookie cutter or any shape cutter
- piping bag

1 Put the chia seeds in a bowl and stir in 3 tbsp water. Soak for 5–10 mins until gloopy. Put the flour into a bowl and rub in the coconut oil until it's almost disappeared. Stir in the spices.

2 In another bowl, mix the sugar, maple syrup, chia mixture and 2 tbsp water until smooth then pour over the flour. Stir to combine, then knead together to make a soft dough. Wrap in cling film until ready to use.

3 Heat the oven to 180C/160C fan/gas 4. Roll out the dough on a lightly floured surface and cut into gingerbread people (or whatever shape you like) and bake for 10–12 mins on baking sheets lined with parchment until just starting to darken at the edges. Cool for a few minutes, then transfer to a rack.

4 Whip the aquafaba using electric beaters until really foamy. Add ¾ of the icing sugar and whisk until smooth and thick, then whisk in the rest of the sugar and the lemon juice until the mixture forms stiff peaks. Transfer to piping bag, snip off the end and use to create designs and faces on your gingerbread.

Nutrition per serving
energy 315 kcals, fat 10g, saturates 9g, carbs 52g, sugars 36g, fibre 1g, protein 2g, salt 0.01g

Gluten-free peanut butter cookies

With just four ingredients, these simple gluten-free peanut butter cookies will delight kids and grown-ups alike..

 PREP 15 mins COOK 12 mins  MAKES 16

- 200g peanut butter (crunchy or smooth is fine)
- 175g golden caster sugar
- ¼ tsp fine table salt
- 1 large egg

1 Heat the oven to 180C/160C fan/gas 4 and line two large baking trays with parchment.
2 Measure the peanut butter and sugar into a bowl. Add ¼ tsp fine table salt and mix well with a wooden spoon. Add the egg and mix again until the mixture forms a dough.
3 Break off cherry tomato-sized chunks of dough and place, well-spaced apart, on the trays. Press the cookies down with the back of a fork to squash them a little. The cookies can now be frozen for 2 months. Cook from frozen adding an extra min or 2 to the cooking time.
4 Bake for 12 mins, until golden around the edges and paler in the centre. Cool on the trays for 10 mins, then transfer to a rack and cool completely. Store in a cookie jar for up to 3 days.

Nutrition per serving
energy 126 kcals, fat 7g, saturates 2g, carbs 12g, sugars 11g, fibre 0.5g, protein 4g, salt 0.2g

Vegan salted caramel biscuit bars

A healthier take on one of our favourite chocolate bars, these biscuits are packed with wholesome ingredients, and free from refined sugar and dairy.

 PREP 45 mins + setting COOK 15 mins   MAKES 18

FOR THE BISCUIT BASE
- 80g porridge oats
- 20g ground almonds
- 50ml maple syrup
- 3 tbsp coconut oil, melted

FOR THE CARAMEL FILLING
- 125g medjool dates , pitted
- 1½ tbsp smooth peanut butter or almond butter
- 2 tbsp coconut oil, melted
- ½ tbsp almond milk
- generous pinch of salt

FOR THE TOPPING
- 150g dairy-free dark chocolate

1 Heat the oven to 180C/160C fan/gas 4 and line a large baking tray with parchment.
2 For the base, blitz the oats in a food processor until flour-like. Add the remaining ingredients and whizz until it clumps. Roll out and cut into 18 (9 x 2cm) rectangles. Place on the tray and neaten with a palette knife. Bake for 10 mins until golden at the edges, then cool.
3 Meanwhile, put all the caramel ingredients in the processor (no need to rinse) and blitz until it forms smooth, shiny clumps. Using a spatula push together, then roll into 18 balls.
4 Squash the caramel onto the cooled biscuits, using your fingers to press it into shape and smooth out bumps, especially on the edges.
5 Melt the chocolate in a microwave or heatproof bowl set over a pan of simmering water. Dip each biscuit in the chocolate, turning with a palette knife. Use a spoon to drizzle over more chocolate, letting the excess drip into the bowl, then chill on the tray for 30 mins or until set. Will keep in an airtight container in the fridge for 5 days.

Nutrition per serving
energy 137 kcals, fat 8g, saturates 5g, carbs 13g, sugars 8g, fibre 0.2g, protein 2g, salt 0.1g

Gluten-free crisp orange shortbread

These simple two-step shortbread are simple to make yet buttery and crumbly. You won't even realise that they're gluten free.

 PREP 10 mins + chilling COOK 15 mins   MAKES 10

- 100g butter, softened
- 50g golden caster sugar
- grated zest ½ orange
- 175g gluten-free flour
- ½ tsp gluten-free baking powder

1 Heat the oven to 190C/fan 170C/gas 5. Lightly oil a baking sheet. Beat the butter, then cream it with the sugar and orange zest until light. Stir in the flour and baking powder and mix to form a dough.

2 Divide the mixture into 10 balls and arrange on a baking sheet. Press each ball flat with the tip of a round-bladed knife. Chill for 15 mins, then bake for 12–15 mins until light golden. Leave on the baking sheet for 2 mins before releasing with a palette knife. Slide onto a rack to cool. Will keep stored in an airtight container for up to a week.

Nutrition per serving
energy 154 kcals, fat 9g, saturates 5g, carbs 20g, sugars 5g, fibre 1g, protein 1g, salt 0.2g

Gluten-free zimtsterne (cinnamon stars)

A version of these German spiced cookies – they're chewy and crisp, similar to an almond macaron and gluten free too!

 PREP 30 mins COOK 15 mins MAKES about 30

- 2 large egg whites
- 1 tsp lemon juice, plus zest 1 lemon
- 200g icing sugar, plus extra for dusting
- 250g ground almonds
- 2 tsp ground cinnamon
- 1 tsp ground ginger

YOU WILL NEED

- 1 x 5cm star-shaped cookie cutter

1 Heat the oven to 150C/130C fan/gas 2 and line a large baking tray with parchment. Whisk the egg whites with an electric mixer until foamy. Add the lemon juice and whisk again until they hold soft peaks.

2 Slowly mix in the icing sugar and whisk until the mixture is stiff. Set aside about a quarter of the mixture. Put the almonds, cinnamon, ginger and zest in the bowl with the meringue and mix to form a stiff, slightly sticky dough.

3 Put the dough on a piece of parchment lightly dusted with icing sugar and dust the top of the dough with sugar, too. Place a second sheet of parchment on top and roll out to ½ cm thick. Peel off the top sheet of parchment and cut out cookies. Place on your baking tray.

4 Use the reserved meringue to cover the tops of the cookies – you may need to add a few drops of water to make it easier to spread. Bake for 12–15 mins until the meringue is set but not browned. Cool fully before storing in sealed container for up to 2 weeks.

Nutrition per serving
energy 78 kcals, fat 5g, saturates 0g, carbs 7g, sugars 7g, fibre 1g, protein 2g, salt 0g

Index